MW00710508

Divine Diva

Other Books by this Author

Reaching The Summit

The Jeweled Path

Coming Home

Road Queens

Divine Diva

by

Catherine MacDonald

Divine Diva
All Rights Reserved © 2007 by Catherine MacDonald

No part of this book may be reproduced or transmitted in any form
or by any means, electronic or mechanical, including photocopying,
recording, or by information storage and retrieval system except by a
reviewer who may quote brief passages in a review to be printed in a
magazine or newspaper without written permission from the publisher
and the author.

This book is a work of fiction. Names, characters, places and incidents
are either products of the author's imagination or are used fictitiously.
Any resemblance to actual events or locales or persona, living or dead, is
entirely coincidental

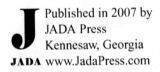

Published in 2007 by
JADA Press
Kennesaw, Georgia
JADA www.JadaPress.com

ISBN: 978-0-9788724-2-7
0-9788724-2-8

Library of Congress Number
LCCN: 2007923441

Cover Design by Mythic Design Studio
http://www.mythicstudio.com/

Interior Design by BookMakers Ink
http://www.bookmakersink.com/

Printed in the United States of America

There is a vitality,
a life force,
an energy
that is translated
through you into action;
and because
there is only one
of you in
all of time,
this expression
is unique.
And if you block it,
it will never exist through
any other medium
and will be lost.

Martha Graham

Prologue

Sue Clark squeezed past the large woman wearing the green pants and slid into her seat. Sue was peeved. She should have reminded her assistant to reserve an aisle seat. Her long legs would be cramped the entire flight. She fastened her seatbelt and rummaged through her briefcase for her assignment. There it was. She put on her glasses and swore. She was being sent into the desert of Arizona, of all the god-awful places, to interview some artist who had written a book that was number ten on the New York Times Bestseller List.

This woman, Sophia Roberts, had written a story that persuaded fifty-something women from all walks of life to follow some funky path and reclaim their divine diva. Whatever that was? She didn't understand anything about life, or people, or the west coast. Were they all crazy out there? Is that what happens when your body soaks up too much sun and you eat too much tofu? What would make educated women abandoned their jobs, families, and responsibilities and head out to the desert north of Sedona, Arizona on the summer solstice each year? Didn't they know it was hot? And heat made hot flashes worse? She knew all about hot flashes, but she finally had them under control. She was now taking hormones and she felt much better. Maybe that was the problem with these women. They all needed to be on hormones.

Sue examined the glossy photos that someone had taken the year before. The photos depicted middle-aged women dancing around a large fire wearing purple gowns and waving golden wands. She read the caption: *"Each year at the Goddess Festival in the desert north of Sedona, thousands of women participate in this mid-course correction for the year by reclaiming their divine divas, throwing their fears and worries into the great fire pit, and looking forward to the future."*

Sue grimaced. Of all the stupid things. What happened if your gown caught on fire?

She was angry with her editor. Kyle knew she had little patience for New Age hoopla, but he sent her anyway because he was covering a *real* news story about the congressman from Virginia's illicit affair with an intern. She would have killed for that story.

The flight attendant demonstrated the safety procedures, and Sue recalled the other times she had been sent west. Once she had interviewed a woman from Seattle who claimed Big Foot impregnated her, another woman who had tended a garden high in the Santa Cruz Mountains allegedly planted by aliens from another galaxy, and once a madam at one of the brothels outside Reno. There had to be something in the water out west.

The jet moved away from the terminal. She reached into her briefcase for the little book that had started this diva revolution and opened to the first page. She could easily finish this by the time the plane touched down in Phoenix.

Chapter 1

It was unseasonably warm for early March. The balmy air hung like a thick blanket over the valley. Sophia lugged the groceries into the kitchen and set them on the granite counter.

The red light winked on the answering machine. "I have a business meeting tonight and I think it's going to be a long one, so don't wait up. Katie called my office again. She needs more money. If you'd leave your cell phone on, she could get a hold of you and not bother me at work. You *do* realize how busy I am right now with this big case." Brad's voice ended abruptly.

Sophia stared at the bags of groceries. *Shit!* Another long night alone. Brad seemed to be working longer and longer hours. And when he was home, the two of them sat in the living room and stared at each other while the TV droned in the background. She had tried to participate in his life. She'd even taken up golf—something she had sworn she would never play. But it seemed that no matter how hard she tried, even spending hours at the driving range, taking those stupid lessons and being his partner in several best ball tournaments, her game wasn't good enough for him, so she quit. Besides—golf was for old people and she wasn't that old—yet.

After unloading the groceries she'd bought for a special meal she had discovered in one of those magazines that lined the checkout counter, she took a deep breath. She was trying to make the marriage work. Even her counselor agreed that she was doing every thing she could. When the food was placed in the refrigerator, Sophia went upstairs to change clothes. It had been a long day at the office, and she couldn't wait to get out of that confining linen suit.

A note, written in childish handwriting by Mrs. Hernandez, sat on the polished hall table. "I be late next week. My daughter goes to the baby doctor. Lemon oil, bleach, trash liners." *I don't even know why we need a housekeeper,* Sophia thought. *There's rarely anyone home.*

She stripped off her clothes and stepped into the shower. The strong smell of bleach and cleanser assaulted her nose, but a washcloth soaked with almond body wash helped disguise the pungent odor and scrubbed the day away. As the warm water fell on her face, she closed her eyes and wished she could stay right there forever. She hated selling real estate—or, attempting to. She hadn't sold anything lately and that wasn't helping her marriage. When their daughter, Katie, left for college, Sophia thought that would give her and Brad more time together, but it hadn't. He seemed to be away from home even more now since Katie had left. The ringing of the phone stunned her thoughts. After grabbing a towel and dribbling water on Mrs. Hernandez's clean floors, she managed an out-of breath, "Hello."

"What took you so long, Mom?"

"I was in the shower."

"Dad said you'd call when you got home. Isn't it like six-thirty? Where have you been?" Katie's high pitched voice grated on her nerves. Sophia pictured her daughter tapping her foot impatiently and twisting her long blond hair.

"I needed a shower first." *Why am I explaining myself to my daughter?*

Katie sighed. "Whatever. I need some money—like tonight. I had to pay a lab fee and we're going shopping this weekend. I need a new outfit for the spring dance."

"Didn't you just buy clothes two weeks ago?"

"Mom, everyone's seen them. I can't wear something old to this dance. What century were you born in? You don't want me to look like a reject, do you? People dress down here and I have to look good. I do have my reputation to think about."

Sophia started to argue but decided it was easier to write the check. She knew Brad would. *That was the problem with Katie,* she decided, as she listened to her chatter on about how expensive college life was and never having enough money. "Okay. I'll put a couple of hundred dollars into your account tomorrow, but that's it until next month. Dad and I have two college tuitions to pay for. Ben manages on the money we send him. Why can't you?"

"That's because he wears the same old thing every day. It's different for a girl. It's not like I'm buying four hundred dollar shoes. Got to go, Mom. Going to the library to study for an English test tomorrow. Love you." Katie hung up.

Sophia hugged the towel tightly around her body. No, Katie wasn't buying four hundred dollar shoes, just four hundred dollar purses. The last time she was home she carried one of those Prada purses. Sophia didn't even own a Prada purse. She bought hers on the clearance rack.

Almost dry after the conversation, Sophia fluffed her hair with the towel, then wiped the water from the floor. *Where did I go wrong? I tried to be the perfect mother, always there for my children.* They had taken the right lessons, attended the best summer camps, belonged to the right gym, and took the proper courses in high school to get into the colleges of their choice. *I never missed a sports event, and often wiped their tears when Brad missed their games because of a trial or business trip.* Her diligence had paid off. Ben had been accepted early to the University of Colorado at Boulder, where he skied on the team. Katie had been accepted to University of Southern California, Brad's alma mater.

Sophia slid into her favorite pair of jeans, the ones Brad hated, and reached for a tee shirt from the piles of clean laundry Mrs. Hernandez had folded. *Well, if he isn't going to be home for dinner then there's no way I'm cooking!*

Her stomach growled as she padded downstairs and pulled out the list of take-out menus she kept in a drawer by the phone. Chinese, pizza, chicken, sushi—the possibilities were endless. Toward the back of the stack, she found the one for the new Thai restaurant Brad had raved about. She liked Thai, the spicier the better. She called the restaurant and placed her order.

"Thirty minutes," the young girl said. "Seventeen dollars and ninety-seven cents."

"Thank you." Sophia set the phone down and picked up the newspaper to scan the local news. Nothing new—the standard robberies and petty crimes. *What was it with people?* Needing to find new listings to generate sales, she searched the real estate section, and studied the listings that were for sale by owner. Brad had insisted that she produce some income to off-set their expenses. The irony was she wasn't the big spender—he was and he spent money like it flowed from the sink. Over her protests, he had purchased the new house, the red Porsche, and had his suits made exclusively by an Italian guy in Las Vegas. He even paid fifty thousand dollars to join the country club so he could play golf with the *right* people. She walked around the house, turned the lights on as she entered each room, then picked up her purse and headed to the garage.

The restaurant was several miles away and the parking lot was filled, so she parked in the alley. The place bustled with energy as she maneuvered her way through the people to the podium. "Take-out for Sophia," she told the young Asian woman.

"I see if it's ready," the woman said. "Wait here." She darted into the kitchen.

Sophia stretched her neck and glanced around the crowded restaurant. Tucked into the back corner, she saw a man who resembled her husband, and a young woman who looked vaguely familiar, hunched over a table. They were whispering and holding hands. She reached into her purse and found her glasses. Her eyes widened as she stared at the couple. *Isn't that Brad? And isn't that Leslie?* Her stomach lurched as the man turned his head towards the counter. *It is him and he isn't working.* Her chest felt like shattered glass as she stared at the couple. Unable to control herself, she stormed over to the table. "So, Brad, this is your late meeting, huh?"

Brad dropped Leslie's hands. "It's not what you think, Sophia. We were just discussing a case."

"And I'm the Queen of England!" Sophia's heart hammered as she felt a murderous rage sweep through her body. "How could you, Leslie? I helped you find your apartment. I had you over to the house for dinner. I treated you like one of my own children."

Leslie shrank in her chair. "We never meant to hurt you. It just happened."

Sophia picked up both glasses of water and poured them over their heads. "You professed to be my friend and all the time you were scheming after my husband. You little slut!"

"Jesus, Sophia! What do you think you're doing?" Brad whispered. "You're making a fool out of yourself in this restaurant." He looked ridiculous with water running down his face, staining his expensive suit. Leslie's expertly applied makeup was streaked.

"That's appropriate, Leslie," Sophia said. "Now you look exactly like what you are, Leslie—a disgusting drowned rat!"

Brad wiped his face with a napkin. "There's no need to make a scene, Sophia. I was going to tell you about us. I was just waiting for the right time." He handed Leslie a napkin. "Here, sweetheart. I'm sorry."

Leslie wiped her face and stood. "I'm going home, Brad. I'll see you tomorrow."

Sophia pushed Leslie down in her chair. "Don't bother on my account. I'm leaving, so you can continue with your tawdry affair." She glared at her husband. "You should be ashamed of yourself. She's not much older than your son."

Wanting to leave the restaurant in a hurry, Sophia almost forgot to pick up her take-out order. She rushed back to the counter.

"Is everything okay?" the young woman asked. "Here is your food."

Sophia glanced at the bill. "That man over there is going to pay my bill," she said pointing to Brad. "He'll give you a nice tip." She added twenty dollars to the total. "Thank you for your trouble."

The woman smiled. "Thank you, Miss. I give him the check right now." The woman headed over to Brad's table.

After leaving the restaurant as quickly as she could, Sophia heard a voice just as she got close to her car. "Hey, can you spare some change, lady?"

She turned around and saw a man with long stringy hair pushing a shopping cart filled with black plastic bags. "You'll have to wait for my husband if you want change. He's in the restaurant eating dinner with his little slut. But have my dinner. I've lost my appetite." She handed the bag to the man.

He peered inside and scratched his head. "Hey, thanks. I haven't eaten today."

Sophia forced her tears away. "You're welcome. Have a good night." She walked to her car, started the engine, and quickly drove out of the parking lot. She couldn't hold back the tears any longer. "Damn you," she cried. "You pig—you asshole! And you had to pick a child!"

* * *

"I'm not coming in today," she explained to her broker over the phone. "I've got some horrible flu bug, and I was up all night. I don't want anyone else to get it, so I'll work from home," she lied.

"Take it easy, Sophia," Cort said. "Quite a few people in the office have had this bug. Lay low, and if anything pops up, I'll give you a call."

"Thanks. I appreciate it." Sophia hung up and stared out the living room window. It was a beautiful day. The remaining snow glistened off Mount Rose while the daffodils stretched their slender necks towards the sun. She picked up the newspaper. The forecast called for a strong winter storm by evening.

Emotionally exhausted, she flopped on the couch and stared at the photo taken of the four of them when Katie had been fifteen and Ben seventeen. The happy family grinned at her, immortalized in pressed white shirts and denim jeans. She glanced down at her hands and her eyes froze on the same quarter carat diamond ring Brad had placed on her finger twenty-three years before when he had asked her to marry him. She stared at her hands. These were the hands of a woman who lived, not like the long lacquered nails of Leslie. These were the hands of a mother, a wife, a homemaker, and a gardener. She remembered Brad offering to buy her a larger diamond several years before, but she had declined because she was partial to the little gold ring with the small diamond.

Brad's red Porsche screamed into the driveway. She heard his key unlock the front door, and he walked into the living room. "I didn't want you to find out like this, Sophia. I am truly sorry. I just fell in love with her."

"Why?"

"I don't know. She's so uncomplicated."

"What the hell is that supposed to mean?"

He shrugged. "She makes me feel young again."

"You're just having a mid-life crisis. That's all. It'll pass. Don't you remember when this happened to Linda and Dan? They went to counseling and they were able to repair their marriage."

"We're already in counseling," he reminded her, "and I'm not Dan. I don't want to repair our marriage. We've been going to that counselor for the last two years. It hasn't helped." His voice grew husky. "I don't want to hurt you. You've been a wonderful mother. The kids have turned out great."

"You have hurt me," she whispered. She was not going to let him get off this easy.

Brad nodded. "I am so sorry. It was never my intention. I'll be fair. I promise."

"So that's it? You just want to call it quits after all these years. Slam, bam, thank you, Ma'am, Sophia. I've found someone younger and sexier. A child who makes me feel like I'm thirty again."

He shook his head and walked towards the stairs. "I'm going to pick up a few things. I'll just be a moment. Please call my office and let my secretary know when you're going to be away for a few hours. I'll arrange to have the rest of my things picked up."

Sophia followed him to the base of the stairs. "You're moving in with Leslie?"

"For the moment. After we sell the house, we'll look for something together."

"You're moving into the same apartment I helped her find and decorate? How ironic!"

He looked sad. "I've got to get back to the office. I am sorry you had to find out like this, but it's better that you know. I'm too old to be sneaking around."

"Well, I'm glad your conscience won't bother you any longer. I wouldn't want that." She glared at him. "What about the children? Who's going to tell them?"

He turned and started up the stairs. "Could you?"

"No!" she screamed. "I'm not the one who has been whoring around, Counselor. You have ten minutes to get your things. If you're not out by then, I'm going to call the cops." She stormed into the kitchen.

As she heard the sound of footsteps and drawers opening and closing, she burst into tears. "I've become my mother," she sobbed. She wiped her tears with her shirt sleeve. She still heard movement upstairs. How were the children going to react to the news? What was going to happen to her? Finally she heard him coming down the stairs.

"I've got all I need for now," he said.

She walked into the foyer and saw him standing stone-still, holding two suitcases. "I just bought those for our trip next month to Costa Rica, which it looks like we're not taking," she said. "You're not taking them both?"

"I'll return one later. I don't have anything else to put my things in."

"Plastic bags would serve you right. Now get out of my house!"

"It's still my house, too," he said softly. "We're going to have to put it on the market soon. I need the money. I am sorry, Sophia." He walked towards the front door.

"If you think I'm going to be reasonable about this, you're crazy!" she yelled. "I'm going to tell the children the truth. You're a lying, cheating, sack of shit. I'm not selling the house. Our children need a house to come home to, and I don't want to move."

He opened the door and turned around. "I never meant to hurt you. It just happened." He closed the door and casually walked away from her and their marriage.

Sophia sat in front of the vanity mirror and gazed at her reflection. Faint lines resonated from blue eyes; gray hairs intermingled with blond. She squinted and saw a few spider veins on her right cheek. Her teeth needed whitening. *Is this why he left,* she wondered?

She thought about the irony of life. Her father had left her mother fifteen years ago for a much younger woman. Her mother hired an expensive divorce lawyer, sued her father for everything he had, and got just about all of it. She took the money and purchased a luxurious home in Palm Springs, where she spent the winter months. Summers she spent at her condo in Laguna Beach.

She thought about calling her friend Amy, but remembered she was vacationing in Hawaii with her husband. She sniffled as she reflected on Amy's marriage. Her children had graduated college and were self-supporting, and now Amy and Steve traveled frequently and enjoyed life. Last September, Amy had suggested that she and Brad join them in France, but he had refused because he said he had a big case coming to trial and he couldn't leave. The big case was obviously Leslie. She stared at the clock. It was only ten. The vacant day stretched out in front of her.

Chapter 2

"I thought you were sick, Sophia," Cort said as he shuffled a stack of papers on his cluttered desk.

"I just stopped by to pick up a few phone numbers," she said. "I'm going to make some calls from home."

Cort leaned back in his chair and cleared his throat. "There's no easy way to say this, so I'm just going to blurt it out. I want you to know that this comes from upper management, and it's not my decision." He coughed. "I'm going to have to let you go because of your lack of sales. You know the policy in this office."

Sophia became a rock as she stared at Cort's balding head.

"I'm sorry, Soph. You know how the head office operates. They only want top producers." He studied her with his dark brown eyes. "This can't come as much of a surprise. It's been months since you've sold a property." Then he paused. "You don't look good. Perhaps you should go home and crawl into bed."

She blinked as she wrapped her mind around the situation. "This is fucking unbelievable. You can tell the head office they can go to hell!" She turned and hurried out of the office. She was not going to cry in front of him.

Cort followed her out of the office. "I am sorry, Sophia. I hate to lose you. You brought such energy to the office, but you know how those geeks in the head office are."

She turned around. "I sure do. If you don't sell several million dollars a year and have firm young flesh, then you're history. I know you mean well, but just leave me alone so I can get my things in peace. And don't tell me you're sorry. I've heard enough of that lately."

She hurried to her desk, which was nothing more than a tiny cubicle, and gathered her things. She scooped up the pictures of her children, her calendar, sketchbook, and several plants. After a quick glance around her office, she realized that she wasn't going to miss this place.

"Goodbye, Janet," she said to the secretary who had always been so kind.

"I'm so sorry, Sophia," Janet whispered. "They fired Carol and Sally earlier this morning. They say they're trying to update their image, whatever that means." She lowered her voice. "They just hired several young women who can't be older than thirty. I think I better start looking for another job."

Sophia thought for a moment. Carol and Sally were in their early fifties. "Is that what this is about? Getting rid of women over fifty." She studied Janet, an attractive woman with graying blond hair that she wore swept off her smooth face. Janet was always well-groomed and impeccably dressed. "Isn't this discrimination? They're not firing the men over fifty."

"It sounds that way to me," Janet said, "but they can say your sales were slow."

"Were Carol's and Sally's?"

Janet nodded. "But we've just came through one of the heaviest winters in recent history. Residential real estate has been slow all throughout the city and the surrounding areas. Most of the agents in this office have had slow sales."

Sophia felt the tears threaten. She had never been fired before. "They were happy with my performance last spring and summer. This sucks." She whispered to Janet. "I turn fifty next week."

Janet grabbed her hand. "Listen to me, Sophia. My friends tell me fifty is fabulous. They say that when a woman turns fifty, she blossoms into her own power. That's when she has gained true self-confidence and wisdom. A woman over fifty is enlightened and celebrates her years and wisdom."

Sophia laughed. "They don't want enlightened women around here. They want tight flesh and perky breasts."

Janet smiled softly. "Good luck, Sophia. Keep in touch."

Sophia lifted the cardboard box filled with her things. "Thanks, Janet." She held her head high as she walked out of the office. The wind blew from the west. Dark clouds lingered over the mountains. For once, the weatherman was correct. A storm was blowing in.

"Your dad's not home tonight," she told Ben over the phone. It was later that afternoon, and she was sipping her third cup of coffee.

"Where is he? I need to talk to him."

"He's away on business. Is there something I can help you with?"

"No. It's just a business question. I don't think you'd understand."

Of course not, I'm a woman. She remembered that Brad had kept their financial affairs from her because he thought she just didn't understand. She wasn't stupid. She knew they didn't have as much money as he said they did. She contemplated telling Ben the truth about his dad, but bit her tongue. Brad was the one who had cheated and left the marriage. He would have to tell the children. She asked Ben about his studies, and they chatted for a few minutes. He promised he'd be home soon for a visit. She hung up, stared at the kitchen clock and debated her next move.

An idea surfaced. She went to the study and rummaged around in the top drawer of the maple desk where Brad kept the savings checkbook and the American Express card he only used for special occasions, the one she had been forbidden to ever use. However, now she felt that she had the right to look at anything in her home that she wanted to. What she found was a shock. Several large sums were written for cash. *He must be spending it on Leslie.* She found the credit card tucked in the back of the drawer and slipped it into her pocket. She was going to do some damage.

It was early evening and the traffic was light. She liked shopping in the evenings when the crowds of the day were tucked in front of their TVs watching the latest reality show. Years ago she had discovered that retail therapy took her mind off her troubles. She usually shopped for the children or the house, but tonight she just might run up an obscene amount of charges on herself. Leslie dressed in the latest fashions. Why not her? The last thing she wanted to do was look like some frumpy middle-aged woman. Besides, her fiftieth birthday was next week, and it looked as if she was going to be spending it alone, so she'd buy her own damn present.

Taking notice of what she was wearing, she realized that she was a pitiful sight. She had thrown on stained brown jeans and a beige pullover. Her mother's advice seemed to storm at her. "Middle-aged women should never wear brown, especially those who are large in the behind because you'll look like a baked potato." She remembered her mother's other silly fashion dictates. "One should never wear white after Labor Day. Wear gloves so you won't get age spots. A woman covers her shoulders. Hair should be always perfectly coifed." Sophia ran her fingers through her short blond hair. *There, perfectly coifed.*

That evening the crowds at the mall were light. Sophia wandered around the stores, running her fingers over the fine fabrics. She entered *Elegante*, an exclusive boutique she had often dreamed of shopping in. But tonight, with the American Express card and her fiftieth birthday looming, she decided—why not? Leslie spent money, probably their money, on fancy clothes, makeup, and jewelry. So why not her? She had always shopped at discount stores or department store clearance sales, trying to be frugal for the betterment of her family, and look where it had gotten her. Dumped for a younger, tighter model.

"I'm looking for something wicked and expensive," she told the young sales clerk as she pulled out the card. "Do you take American Express?"

"Of course and with your figure you should have no problem finding something that fits that description. You're about a size two, correct?"

"Usually. It depends on the cut." She didn't want to tell the young girl that no matter how thin one was in middle-age, gravity still prevailed.

The sales girl smiled slightly. "Come this way. I have the most exquisite silk pantsuit that will look stunning on you."

Sophia followed the young woman to the back of the store. She didn't know where she'd wear a silk pantsuit, but if it would run up the card and leave Brad with an enormous bill, then maybe she'd buy two. The young woman held up a hot pink pantsuit with a thick gold belt. Sophia ran her fingers over the cool silk. "This is beautiful. I'd like to try it on, but first I'm going to look around for a few more things."

"I'll put this in a dressing room for you. Take your time." The young woman took the pantsuit, unlocked a dressing room, and hung the suit on a gold-toned hook.

Sophia continued to browse through the racks, choosing sexy outfits like the ones on the covers of the slick catalogs that flooded her mailbox. She gathered her selections and handed them to the young woman.

"Let me know if I can get you something else," she said. "I'll hang these in your dressing room."

"I think I'm ready now." Sophia followed her to the room, closed the door, and undressed. She slipped the pantsuit on, admiring her reflection in the mirror. The hot pink color brought out her blue eyes. The fabric hugged her waist. There was something about an impending divorce that robbed her appetite and she had lost more weight than she realized. She slipped it off and hung it up. It was a possibility. Next she tried on the studded jeans, a low-cut top and matching jacket. She hated to admit it, but she looked fabulous. After she had tried on the remaining outfits she stared at the woman in the mirror and without any warning, burst into uncontrollable tears.

There was a knock at the dressing room door. "Madam, is there something wrong?"

She sniffled. "No. I'm okay." But she was not okay. Another set of fresh tears made their way down her face.

"Let me get my manager," the young woman said. "She'll know what to do."

Sophia opened the door, but the clerk was gone so she slung herself into the chair.

"Can I help you?" an elegant woman asked, entering the dressing room. "I'm Marilyn Thomas, the store manager. Is there a problem with the clothes? Do you need another size or color?"

Sophia sniffled. "It's not the clothes. I'll take them all, just to spite him. I thought buying expensive clothes and sticking him with the bill would make me feel better, but it doesn't." She wiped her nose. "I'm such a failure. My marriage is over. My kids are away at college. I just got fired, and I turn fifty next week." She glanced at the older woman standing in front of her who was dressed in black silk pants and a deep purple sweater. A silver pendant adorned her neck and large silver loops dangled from her ears. "I don't know why I'm telling you this. I'm sorry. It's not you problem."

The woman smiled, extending her hand. "Why don't you join me in the office for some tea? I'm not going to send you out into the cold night like this. You can think about the clothes." She turned her head and said to the young woman.

"Brooke, I'm going to be in my office with…" She leaned over and whispered. "What's your name, dear?"

"Sophia. Sophia Roberts."

She smiled. "I'm going to be in the office with Sophia. If you need me, please come and get me." The woman turned to Sophia. "Come with me, dear. I think I can help you."

Sophia followed her into a tiny office. The sound of trickling water from a stone fountain soothed her fragile nerves. The office was filled with healthy green plants and stacks of books. The woman gestured her to sit on the chintz covered loveseat. "I have just the right tea for what ails you. Let me put some water on." She took a brass teapot, filled it with bottled water, and placed it on a hot plate.

"I feel strange talking to a woman I don't know." Sophia took a tissue from her purse and blew her nose. "I'm usually not this emotional."

The woman smiled softly. "Sometimes it's easier to confide in people you don't know because they don't judge you like your friends do." She reached for two earthen mugs. "I think you'll like this tea. I discovered it when I was trekking through Nepal several years ago. It clears the mind and points you in the direction you need to go."

Sophia watched as the woman poured the hot water, steeped two different tea bags, and handed one mug to her. "You don't have the same tea as me."

"The tea I'm giving you has led me all over the world. I've had amazing experiences and met the most fascinating people, but now I need to stay put and help my daughter. Her husband recently left her for a woman he met at the gym." She shook her head slowly. "She has two small children."

"That's horrible. I guess I'm not the only woman with a wandering husband. At least my children are in college. It must be hard on your daughter." Sophia sipped the tea. It had a strange, exotic taste. After several more sips, she felt her anxiety leaving. "I feel better. What's in this tea?"

The woman smiled gently. "Nothing harmful. I promise. This tea was created by a Shaman to help people clear their heads." She laughed. "Don't worry. I didn't poison you." She sipped her tea. "Why don't you tell me what happened between you and your husband?"

Sophia leaned against the plush cushions and stared into the mug. What really had happened between them? Was there an actual date or event that she could point to? She shrugged, staring at the woman. What was her name again? She thought for a moment. Maureen, no it was Marilyn. She gazed at the woman's dark eyes and saw kindness. "I guess he just fell out of love with me. He's *in love* with this young attorney in his office." She laughed. "It's quite ironical. When she was first hired by his firm, I was the one recruited to help her find an apartment. I went with her to San Francisco to shop for clothes and things for her apartment. I had her over to our house for dinner when she was lonely and missing her own mother, who by the way lives in Cozumel and only sees her twice a year. I had no idea she was after my husband." She paused. "Brad and I had been in counseling for two years. Our fights were escalating, but I never thought it was because of another woman." She wiped her eyes. "Last night I found them holding hands in a restaurant. I confronted them, but do you know what the jerk did?"

Marilyn shook her head and waited for the answer.

"At first he denied it. I don't know what came over me, but I picked up their water glasses and poured them over their heads. You should have seen Leslie. It was hysterical."

"How long have you been married?" Marilyn asked gently.

"Twenty-three years in June." Sophia set the mug down and reached in her purse for another tissue.

"It seems like someone is trying to get your attention," Marilyn said.

"What do you mean?"

"Sometimes we need to find ourselves at the bottom of despair before we make changes that are necessary for growth."

"Are you saying I'm having a mid-life crisis?" Sophia asked. "Brad's the one who's having the crisis. He bought the sports car last year and now has the young girlfriend."

Marilyn smiled gently. "I don't think it's your average mid-life crisis, but more of a crisis of your soul." She studied Sophia. "Is your mother still alive?"

Sophia laughed. "Yes, but she's been the topic of many sessions with my therapist. We have never really gotten along. I don't think she likes me. Oh, she loves me because she's supposed to. She is one of those dutiful mothers— never forgets a birthday or Christmas, but she's incapable of real love or warmth." She laughed. "At least that's what my therapist says."

Marilyn nodded. "My mistake. I thought it was your mother. I'm reading the energy around you, and I see a vibrant woman dressed in a flowing gown painting a beautiful picture. I think she's important to you."

Sophia thought for a moment. "That's my aunt, my mother's sister. She lives in Sedona and is an artist. I haven't seen her in several years because Brad thinks she's crazy and he's forbidden me to see her."

Marilyn smiled. "I suggest you call your aunt and ask if you can come for a visit. The red rocks will heal your injured soul."

"The red rocks?"

Marilyn nodded. "The red rocks surround Sedona. Your soul will find what it needs there and hiking the trails will heal your spiritual wounds. Did you know that walking is an ancient form of pursuing a spiritual path?"

"My husband is leaving me and you're telling me I have to follow some spiritual path." This was confusing to Sophia. She had entered this store to run up her husband's credit card, and now she was being guided into some spiritual path to heal her soul by a woman she had just met.

"It is important that you hike alone. That is the only way the goddesses will find you." Marilyn smiled. "I have a feeling your aunt knows this."

"The goddesses? Like in religion?"

"Yes," Marilyn answered softly.

"I'm sorry. I don't mean to be rude, but I gave up on religion years ago. I was raised Catholic and I had enough mumbo-jumbo religious theory poured down my throat to last for years. My mother and the nuns saw to that." She stared at her mug. "I don't believe in God," she admitted.

Marilyn smiled softly. "But the Goddess of All believes in you. Let me pour you another cup of tea," Marilyn said. "Trust me."

Sophia handed her the empty mug. Marilyn steeped a fresh tea bag and sat patiently while she drank. Suddenly Sophia felt a wave of energy. She saw a flash of white light and a vision of herself hiking through tall, craggy red rocks. The day was warm, the sky brilliant blue, and she felt calm and centered. "What's happening to me?"

"The tea has cleared your mind and pointed you in the direction you need to take. You need to visit your aunt. She will guide you." Marilyn reached for her hand. "You need to reconnect with the divine feminine and awaken your diva power."

"Diva power?" Sophia felt confused. *There had to be something in that tea.* She felt like she was back in the seventies and had done some powerful drug.

"Diva power is a woman's own personal soul path," Marilyn explained. "It is a spiritual transition that occurs at mid-life when a woman gives birth to her own wisdom and creativity and reinvents her life. It is the time when a woman honors her inner desires and sets out to find her true calling. By the time most women celebrate their fiftieth birthday, they have paid their dues to society, raised children, taken care of husbands and aging parents, and put their time on the corporate treadmill. At fifty, it is time for a woman to uncover her authentic self. She is in her prime. This is not your mother's fifties."

"But I'm confused. You said there were goddesses. Is this some kind of pagan religion?"

Marilyn laughed. "The goddesses won't hurt you. They're loving, beautiful, and fun. You'll enjoy them. I promise. They have a sense of humor." She paused and her tone became serious. "Sophia, of the countless women who have made this journey, none has returned unchanged. Open your mind so the wisdom of the Goddess can flow."

There was a knock at the door. The sales clerk stuck her head in. "I'm sorry to bother you, but I have several customers out there."

"I'll be right out." Marilyn stood and smiled warmly at Sophia, then kissed her on the forehead. "You will be protected on your travels, my dear. Goddess Bless."

Chapter 3

Sophia had always experienced dramatic dreams and that night dreamt she was in the backyard barbecuing chicken while her family waited at the picnic table. Suddenly, the sky grew deep purple and the wind blew. A naked man streaked through the backyard screaming, "The world's going to end in fifteen minutes." She yelled for the children to run into the house and assume earthquake positions. Brad sat at the table calmly reading the paper, never glancing up. The ground shook violently. She fell against the table and hit her head. When she awoke, she discovered she was on a jet plane. She glanced around the plane. Brad and the children were nowhere to be seen. An old woman sitting in front of her turned around. The woman grinned, her face a mosaic of fine lines. "You need to wake up and pay attention to your life."

Sophia awoke with a startle and sat up in bed. She rubbed her eyes. The old woman's face was still vivid in her mind. The dream didn't make any sense. *Who was the old woman?*

A shiver swept through Sophia and she wrapped the bedcovers around her body. The dream had seemed so real. She stared at Brad's open closet door. Empty hangers hung, his golf bag was gone. She still couldn't believe it. He had left her for that child.

She reached for the note he had left on the front porch the night before and slowly reread the familiar handwriting. *Please call my office and talk to John. He'll handle everything. I'm sorry you had to find out like that, but we feel it's better that you know. I'm tired of sneaking around. I'd like to buy the house from you. I'll be fair. Brad*

After folding the note and placing it back on the nightstand, her whole body seemed to be numb. Even though she didn't really like the Mediterranean-style house, it was hers. The idea of Leslie sleeping in her bedroom, taking a bath in her marble tub, and cooking meals in her kitchen made her nauseous. She pulled the covers over her head and snuggled down. There was no reason to get out of bed.

Sophia didn't leave the house for days. Her birthday came and went. She spent the day alone, wandering through the house, remembering the years of motherhood and marriage. Her children called and she pretended to be upbeat. "Yes, your dad's taking me to dinner. Yes, he bought me a gift. What? Oh, a nice diamond necklace." The lies seemed to appease the kids because they promptly hung up, secretly happy because they thought their mother was taken care of. When her friends called, she promised she'd meet them for lunch the following week because she was just too busy.

She cried, her moods swinging like the March wind. She tried to read, but the words failed her. Insomnia gripped her. She watched late night movies on cable TV, the cheesy ones that turned out happily-ever-after. She burst into tears during the sappy commercials, then unplugged the TV because the media seemed infatuated with youth. It hit her like a truckload of anti-aging cream. She was old. She was on top of the mountain sliding down quickly into a senior living center.

The phone continued to ring. She tired of its intrusion, so she unplugged it and was left with shattering silence. She wore the same flannel pajamas for days, the ones with the coffee stains on the front and frayed hems. The only time she ventured outside the house was to pick up the mail and paper, and that was after dark. She scanned the paper for news and stumbled upon the obituaries. There staring at her, looking healthy and beautiful, was a woman she had known years before. The paper said she had died of a heart attack and left three children and a husband. A heart attack at fifty-one! *Life wasn't fair.*

After a week, she finally dragged herself out of bed and into the bathroom, determined to finally take a shower because she couldn't stand herself any longer. She stared at her reflection in the mirror. Dark circles were etched under her eyes. Her hair was dirty and limp. Her pajamas hung on her thin frame. Lately, her diet had consisted of saltines and tomato soup.

The night before, she had finally spoken to Brad. He didn't even want to try and reconcile. He wanted a divorce, and he wanted it quickly because he and Leslie were thinking about having a baby. A baby! He already had two kids. Besides, he had never been that enthralled when Ben and Katie were growing up. She couldn't remember if he had ever changed a dirty diaper, and she knew he had never gotten up in the middle of the night with a crying baby!

She stared at her reflection in the mirror. Maybe she should have taken better care of herself. She pulled the skin up on the sides of her face. There, she looked about ten years younger. Perhaps some Botox or collagen treatments like all her friends were having would erase some of the years. Maybe she should hire a personal trainer and sculpt her body to look like Leslie's.

But a little voice in the back of her mind nagged. *It wouldn't bring him back. He's made his choice, and it's not you.*

She knew what she needed to do. She picked up the phone and dialed. "Cassandra's in the studio," the man on the other end said. "Let me get her."

"I don't want to bother her if she's busy," Sophia said.

"Nonsense. She'd love to talk to you. She was just saying at breakfast how nice it would be if you would come down and visit."

Several minutes later her aunt picked up the phone. "Sophia! What a wonderful surprise! I had a dream about you last night. Are you okay?"

"Brad left me for another woman. I don't know what to do."

"I had this unsettling dream last night," Cassandra said. "I saw you standing at the front door with tears running down you face as Brad drove off in a red sports car. I'm sorry, honey. I remember the pain. I tried to call you several days ago to wish you a belated happy birthday, but there was no answer."

"I wasn't taking phone calls."

"That's perfectly understandable. Why don't you come and visit me? We're long overdue for a good, long visit."

Sophia sniffled. "That's one of the reasons I'm calling. I don't want to bother you with my personal problems, but I met this woman in a boutique." Sophia explained the strange tea and the advice Marilyn had given. "I bought the clothes and put it on the American Express card. I don't know where I'll wear them, but it sure felt good at the time."

Cassandra chuckled. "Good for you. Get him where it hurts—right in the wallet. I remember when your father left your mother. She ran up thousands and thousands of dollars on his credit cards. I think your father is still paying them off." Cassandra was silent for a few moments, and then she added, "The woman in the store was right. You need to come to the Red Rocks."

"I just don't understand what makes the Red Rocks so special." Sophia still thought this goddess thing was nothing but a bunch of New Age psychobabble, but she didn't have many options right now.

"Native Americans and other spiritually-enlightened people consider this area to be the spiritual vortex of the Southwest," Cassandra answered quietly.

"Hmm. I remember the last time I was down there you talked about vortexes, but I thought it sounded like a lot of New Age hoopla."

"Every seven minutes Sedona experiences a mini-earthquake," Cassandra said. "You can't feel it, but it registers. This is the Earth letting go its energy and the vortexes amplifying it. The Red Rocks will be a good place for you to release your diva power. Many women around your age have re-examined their lives and completed this journey."

"Marilyn talked about diva power."

"When can I expect you?"

Sophia awoke the following morning shivering and shaking. She had dreamt she had returned home from the grocery store. The house felt strangely empty. She ran around the house, discovering that every picture and memento of her children had vanished. It was as if her years of motherhood only existed in her dreams.

She leaped out of bed and ran to the wall where her shrine hung. Ben and Katie stared back at her in various stages of development. They grinned from their school pictures. They stood with the teams in the sports pictures. They stood next to her in several family photos, and in their graduation portraits they looked as if they were ready to take on the world. She stared at the pictures, leaning against the wall, and exhaled. It had all been a bad dream.

* * *

"I'm leaving tonight," she told her aunt over the phone, "but first I'm going to trade in this grocery-catcher. My carpool days are long over and I need something fun and racy."

"Be bad, honey," Cassandra said. "Call me when you get on the road."

The morning was cool, so she reached for her jacket. The forecaster had predicted rain by the afternoon. She drove the Volvo station wagon to auto row, slowly driving by the car dealerships as she examined her options. There were Jaguars, Mercedes, Fords, Dodges, and BMWs. Leslie drove a silver convertible BMW. Her aunt's words resonated in her mind. *Be bad, honey.* The more she thought about it, the more she decided her aunt was right. She should be naughty. She had played life by the rules her entire life and look where it had gotten her—tossed aside for a younger, tighter model.

Driving past the Volkswagens, she spotted a canary yellow VW bug prominently on display. She had pleaded with Brad to buy her one when they had first come out, but he refused. He argued that they weren't big enough and looked funky. The sixties were long over.

She had always been a little funky. She was the mother who liked to wear a flower tucked in her hair and favored bohemian clothes. Now Brad had chosen Leslie, so she could drive whatever she wanted. She pulled into the parking lot. Two portly salesmen approached her. "I'm just going to look around," she said as she got out of her car.

The younger man shrugged and walked toward the office, but the older one didn't move. "We have some great deals going on. There's a two thousand dollar factory rebate if you buy today."

"Buy what?" she asked. She knew there was a reason she had never gone car shopping with Brad before. She was already irritated.

"Anything on the lot, but the rebate's only good today. What can I show you?" the man asked, running his eyes up and down her body.

She thought he was around her age, with a stomach that hung over his pants and graying black hair. "What's your name?" she asked. He was beginning to repulse her.

"Glenn. Here's my card." He handed her one of those business cards that is made on a computer.

She took the card and shoved it in her pocket. "I'm going to look around by myself. If I find something I like, I'll come and get you. Thank you." She turned and headed in the direction of the shiny VWs. She opened a red convertible's door and slid inside, smelling the familiar new car smell. Leaning back in the leather seat and placing her hands on the steering wheel, she visualized her journey to Sedona. Letting her spirit soar, she would place fresh flowers in the small vase, stack the CD player with her favorite music and open the top. She glanced at the backseat. There was enough room for people to sit. Brad had been wrong.

She got out of the car and yelled, "I'd like to take a test drive in this one."

Glenn hurried over, a look of excitement on his face. "This one's a turbo," he said as he squeezed his body into the passenger's seat and handed her the key.

"Good, because I want to get where I'm going quickly." She started the engine, drove out of the car lot and headed toward the freeway.

Sophia drove away from the car dealership in her red convertible VW bug. She had chosen red because it was the color of power. *Didn't the president wear his red tie when he gave an important speech?* Her cell phone rang. She fumbled in her purse for the damn thing. Where was it? She found it in the bottom under her lipstick and tissue. "Hello," she said into the mouthpiece as she swerved to avoid a car that was pulling out. "Look where you're going," she heard an angry voice shouting at her.

"What's going on with you and Dad?" Katie asked on the other end. "He called me and said he's staying at this woman's house." She sounded as if she had been crying.

Sophia sighed. It was time for the truth. "I'm glad he finally called you. Did he tell you why he's living with that woman?"

"He just said you two had a fight, and she offered him her spare bedroom until you came to your senses."

She laughed. *The jerk!* "I think you better call your dad back and ask him to tell you the truth. He's not sleeping in her spare bedroom."

"I don't understand what's going on."

"I guess one of us is going to have to be the adult." Sophia explained the situation to her daughter.

Katie gasped. "Does Ben know? I can't believe this. My parents are getting a divorce, Dad's sleeping with Leslie, and no one told us. I used to think I was special, because my parents were still together. Now I'm just like every other kid. Have you both thought about us?"

Sophia contemplated adding fuel to the fire and telling Katie about their plan for a baby, but decided against it. "We're still your parents. We love you very much. This had nothing to do with you. Maybe your father will tire of Leslie. Maybe he'll realize he's made a big mistake. I don't know, honey. All I do know is that he hurt me terribly."

"You need to try harder, Mom. Men want mystery and sex. I saw this show on *OPRAH* that was all about that, but that's gross when I think of the two of you doing it. Ben and I are gone now. You should be having sex like twice a day." Katie paused. "You know what your problem is, Mom?"

Sophia gripped the steering wheel. The last thing she wanted was advice from a child who had yet to have a meaningful relationship. "What is my problem?"

"You're always off in your own little world. Your nose is stuck in a book, or you're digging in the garden. I saw another show that said a woman needs to participate in activities that her husband likes."

Sophia bit her lip. *Why doesn't the man ever try to participate in activities that his wife likes? Why is it the woman who always makes the concession?* "I tried golf, but it didn't help. I don't want to talk about it any longer, Katie. I'm upset. I'm leaving for Sedona. You can reach me on my cell."

"You're not staying with Aunt Cassandra? That woman's nutty. I remember the last time we visited her, and she wanted to read my aura."

Sophia wondered what color Katie's aura was. *Black?* "Yes, I am staying with her and no, she's not nutty. She's just..." She hesitated. How could she explain Cassandra? "She's creative and full of energy."

"Full of craziness if you ask me. Don't do anything stupid that you might regret, Mom. Dad may just be having a midlife crisis and come to his senses in a couple of weeks. Do you want me to come home?"

Sophia felt touched. "No, thank you. You need to concentrate on your school work and I need to get away for awhile and clear my head. Maybe things will work out."

"I hope so, Mom. I'll call you tomorrow." She heard the tears in her daughter's voice. "Bye, Mom."

"Bye, Katie." She knew she needed to call Ben before Katie did. She attached her hands-free device to the phone. The last thing she needed was an accident. Traffic stopped, so she placed the call. He answered on the fourth ring. "Did I wake you?"

"No, well, yes. I was studying for a test and I guess I fell asleep. I had a late night. Are you okay? Dad called and said he wasn't staying at home for a few days. Did you two have a fight?"

"I'm sorry, Benny." The childhood name slid out easily and effortlessly. In her mind he was five again, missing his front teeth, his knees scraped from a recent fall. "That's not the entire truth. I guess your father didn't tell you everything."

"What happened? And why isn't the answering machine on?" Ben asked.

"Your father has found someone else he wants to share his life with. Do you remember Leslie from the office? I think you met her last summer."

Ben whistled. "Yeah. She's hot. What does this have to do with her?"

"Your dad and Leslie are *in love*. She makes him feel young and sexy, and they're going to play house together. In my house, if they get their way."

"That's kind of gross, Mom. She's not much older then me. What does she see in an old guy? Did you know, Mom?"

"I didn't have a clue."

"Now I understand why the answering machine isn't picking up and all I got was voice mail on your cell. I was getting worried."

"I didn't want to talk to anyone. I'm sure you understand. I had some thinking to do." She had always felt more comfortable talking to her son than her daughter. Ben never seemed to be in competition with her. He accepted her as she was, while Katie criticized her for breathing.

"I can fly home this weekend, "Ben said. "I'll talk some sense into him."

She loved her son. He was so uncomplicated. "Thanks, but it's not necessary. I'm leaving this afternoon for awhile. I'm going to stay with my aunt in Sedona. You remember Cassandra?"

Ben laughed. "She's a colorful character. It'll be good for you to get away. Maybe Dad will get tired of Leslie and come back home."

"Maybe." But Sophia was beginning to think that she didn't want him back.

"Mom, you're breaking up," Ben said. "Please call me before you leave the house."

"I will, Ben. I love you." But the connection was lost, and she doubted if he had heard her last words. Now that the energy was in motion, she needed to call her mother, but that could wait until she arrived home.

Her mother wasn't in when she called. She was probably on the golf course, or shopping. Sophia left a brief message saying that she was on her way to Cassandra's. For a split second, she debated on stopping in Palm Springs and visiting her, but decided against it. She didn't need her mother's toxic attitude.

After spending the rest of the afternoon packing, she loaded the car, called her insurance agent to switch coverage, and cancelled her dentist appointment. She didn't know how long she was going to be gone, but she wasn't about to rush home for a routine cleaning.

The phone rang off and on throughout the afternoon, but she ignored it and went about her chores. It rang again as she was loading the dishwasher, and not thinking, she picked it up.

"Finally," Brad said. "You don't answer your phone or cell. The answering machine isn't on. How is someone supposed to get a hold of you?"

"Mail."

"Very funny," Brad said. "I need you to come into the office immediately and meet with John so we can get this matter resolved."

She held her breath for a moment and then swallowed. "I can't."

"What do you mean you can't? The marriage is over. We need to go forward."

"I'm leaving and I don't have the time. You'll have to wait until I return."

"Where are you going?"

"I don't have to tell you. I don't answer to you any more."

"I demand to know. I'm your husband."

"I didn't think you wanted that title anymore. You want to give it to Leslie."

He sighed. "I'm sorry, Sophia. I still care about you. I don't want to make this any harder on you than I already have."

"For your information, you have destroyed my life and our family. I'm going away for awhile because I need to clear my head. You've dumped your torrid affair on me. You didn't tell the children the truth, and now you want the house so you can move that woman into my bedroom and have her sleep in my sheets. Don't you think that's tacky? What would your mother say if she was alive?"

"Leave my mother out of it," he said in a low voice.

"I'll tell you what she would have said. She'd tell you to suck it up and be a man." Sophia couldn't help letting out a hearty laugh before saying, "She'd call you a girlie-man."

"That's enough, Sophia." His tone grew angrier.

"I'm going to hang up, but I want you to know I told the children the truth."

"Why?"

"Because they're adults, and they have a right to know that their beloved father is a cheating bastard."

"Ouch, that hurt." He was silent for a few seconds. "But I guess I deserved it."

"You deserve a whole bunch more." She thought for a moment. "If there's an emergency you can reach me at my aunt's, but don't bother me unless it's urgent. This impending divorce is not urgent."

"Cassandra can't be good for you," Brad said. "She'll cast a spell on you."

Sophia laughed. "No. I think she'll reserve that for you because you're such a pig. Perhaps I'll bring something of yours to help her find the perfect spell for an adulterer. You better not move that little wife-stealing hussy of yours in here until I come back, and we decide together what we're going to do. I don't want that tramp in my home." She slammed the phone down.

A quick glance at the clock showed her that it was almost five. Feeling certain that Brad would rush home and try to prevent her from leaving, she needed to get out of there and on the road quickly.

Her professionally decorated showplace felt cold and uninviting as she walked through, glancing around to see if there was anything else she needed. She had never liked this house. Her heart still resided in the small two-story home they had raised Ben and Katie in. She had loved that house with its lush garden and friendly neighbors. She missed her light-filled studio where she had spent hours painting. The new house was sterile. Brad wouldn't let her use one of the empty rooms as a studio because he was afraid she'd splatter paint on the white carpeting. *Who wanted to live in a house with white carpeting?* He had been adamant about the carpeting, along with everything else. She had argued that she would cover the floor in plastic, but he had moved all her paints to the garage. It was hard to paint in the cold garage.

"Don't gather too much dust for Mrs. Hernandez," she told the house as she closed the front door and hurried down the walkway.

As she drove toward the freeway, she spied a red Porsche speeding in the direction of the house.

Chapter 4

Large silver trucks zoomed past Sophia as she drove on the road to Las Vegas, shaking the small car. She gripped the steering wheel. The highway between Reno and Las Vegas was a two-lane road that traversed the imposing mountains. Her eyes felt heavy as she struggled to focus on the winding road. The sky was inky black. There wasn't even a hint of the moon. She glanced at the dashboard clock and realized she should reach Tonopah soon. Then she would get a room and sleep. God, she was tired. It was as if the last month had finally caught up with her. Finally, she spied the faint lights of Tonopah, Nevada, located in the hills of the San Antonia Mountains, exactly halfway between Reno and Las Vegas. She remembered the history of the town. In the 1800's a miner had accidentally discovered rich silver ore, and his discovery turned the sleepy little town into a bustling city.

She slowed as she approached the city limits. The mining boom was long over and most of the casinos were boarded up. It appeared as if the town had dried up along with the mining. She drove to the south end of town, where the Ramada Inn was located, next to the one grocery store and the local McDonald's. She hoped that on a Wednesday night it would be easy to get a room. In her haste to get out of town before he came to the house, she had forgotten to call and book a room.

"That'll be twenty-nine dollars," the woman behind the desk said briskly. Her chubby, friendly face was prominent with her gray hair upswept in a bouffant. "You're lucky. You got the last room tonight. The dining room closes in an hour." Sophia wondered what brought people to this isolated part of the state on a Wednesday night. She glanced around the lobby, which was decorated with bunnies and eggs. "Miss," the woman said.

"I'm sorry," Sophia said, with a slight blush caused by her mind rambling in so many directions. "Here's my credit card." She handed the woman the American Express card, determined to charge as much as she could before he cancelled it. "Could I have a wake-up call for eight?"

The woman nodded, jotting down the time on a slip of paper. She ran the card and handed her a key. "Have a nice stay."

Sophia smiled and grabbed her overnight bag. She heard the jingle-jangle of slot machines and the squeals of patrons echo through the Victorian-themed hotel. She lugged her bag up the flight of stairs, found her room, and threw the suitcase on the bed. A quick glance around the room, with its red and gold décor, reminded her of a bordello in the late eighteen hundreds. *It's only for one night*, she thought as she headed downstairs toward the restaurant. A young girl led her to a table by the window and handed her a tall laminated menu that offered everything from pancakes to sirloin steak. "I'll be right back to take your order," she said.

"Could I have a glass of red wine?" Sophia asked.

"I'll send the cocktail waitress right over. Our special tonight is chicken fried steak, mashed potatoes, served with a garden salad, and your choice of dressing." She smiled and turned to the next booth.

Sophia leaned against the torn vinyl cushions and stared out the window. Trucks roared through town, their headlights streaming through the restaurant windows. *How did young girls survive in a town that had decayed years ago? Where did they go on Friday nights? Even the drive-in had closed. Perhaps they stole liquor from their parents' cabinets and headed into the hills.* She smiled as she remembered the times in high school she had siphoned whiskey from her mother's bottle and taken it to the football games.

"Did you want a cocktail?"

She glanced up and saw a woman who had to be in her seventies, thin as a willow, with long brown hair, obviously dyed, and heavy makeup. "A glass of your house merlot, please."

The woman scribbled the order on a tablet and grinned. She was missing her top front teeth. "I'll be back in a moment. I have to take that table's order, too," the woman said pointing to a large booth in the corner filled with burly men wearing flannel shirts and baseball caps.

"No rush. I don't have anywhere I have to go."

The elderly waitress hurried off. The younger waitress delivered an order to the booth next to Sophia and then approached her. "Are you ready to order?"

"I haven't even looked at the menu." Sophia picked it up and studied her choices. "I'll have the chef's salad and a cup of chicken noodle soup." She handed the waitress the menu, thinking there shouldn't be much harm in that.

"It'll be just a few minutes." The waitress hurried off.

The elderly cocktail waitress returned and set the glass of wine down. "Enjoy it, honey."

"Thank you." The wine, which wasn't as bad as she expected, began to release a calming effect and allowed her to reflect on her new status. Only a month before, she and Brad had gone out to a nice restaurant, enjoyed a meal, hadn't argued, and gone home and made love. Obviously he had been sleeping with Leslie, too. What about diseases? Should she get a test? Where would she go to get one? Had he compared her body against Leslie's? There was no way a fifty-year-old woman could compare to one in her late twenties.

She felt so stupid. Now that she thought about it, there had been the familiar clues. She had just been too dense to recognize them. About a year before, he had started wearing younger clothes. He changed his cologne to a fragrance advertised for men looking for romance. He whistled as he puttered in the garage. He had never whistled in all their years of marriage. And there was the all important sign—all those late nights at the office. Years ago Cassandra had warned her against marrying him. "It is written in the stars," she told her on her wedding day. "He's not the match for you."

But Sophia had been eager to marry. Her first marriage had ended after only a year. She had made the mistake of marrying the first boy who had asked her father for her hand. They were married in an elaborate ceremony at her parents' country club. He took a job with an insurance company. They lived for several months in the Bay Area, and then he was transferred to Reno. One night over spaghetti and a cheap bottle of Chianti he told her he was gay. The strange thing was that she wasn't at all shocked; in fact, she had always wondered, but Brian had been her ticket away from her mother. She smiled as she thought of Brian. She still cared about him. He lived in San Francisco with his life partner, Scott. They owned and operated a quaint Italian restaurant in North Beach. She still spoke to Brian several times a month and she realized she needed to call and tell him. She knew what he'd say. "Brad was never good enough for you."

The young waitress served her meal. She poked at the processed meat and cheese. What did she expect in the middle of Nevada? A gourmet meal? She ate the low-calorie items, but pushed the soup away. The thick layer of oil floating over the soggy noodles was less than appetizing.

The elderly cocktail waitress returned and picked up her empty glass. "Do you want something else?"

"I'll have another glass of wine since I'm not driving. I'm only walking upstairs."

The waitress set her tray down and slid into the booth across from Sophia. "Where are you headed, honey? It's not safe for a woman to be traveling by herself."

Sophia studied the woman, wondering what quirk of fate had landed her in this place where the tumbleweeds blew across the harsh landscape, and the lawn ornaments were broken down cars. "I'm on my way to visit my aunt. I'm making a few changes in my life."

"Did the son-of-a-bitch leave you?"

"Am I that transparent?"

The waitress smiled. "Only because I've walked that road, honey. More times than I care to count. The last jerk moved me here thirty years ago and then left me with three screaming kids in a double-wide in the hills back there. Look at me. I'm still here." She patted Sophia's hands. "You take care of yourself, you hear. And don't worry about the wine. It's on the house. Scorned women have to stick together." She leaned across the table. "Get him for everything he's worth." She winked, picked up her tray, and left.

Sophia drank her wine in silence, paid her bill, left a large tip, and then headed toward the casino. When she had first moved to Nevada, she and Brian enjoyed gambling and seeing the shows. She liked the energy, the games, and the chance to win. Exchanging a ten dollar bill for quarters and choosing a slot machine was fun. Perhaps Lady Luck would be on her side again. She needed some kind of luck.

Several hours later she trudged up the stairs to her room. She was thirty-five dollars ahead. She tucked the money into her purse, stripped off her clothes, slipped into the clean sheets, and quickly fell asleep.

That night Sophia dreamt she was in labor. A kind nurse wiped her forehead and told her to concentrate on her breathing because soon it would be time to push. The pain gripped her body, and she screamed. The nurse examined her and scooted her up. Sophia gritted her teeth, grunted, and pushed with all her strength. Nothing happened. She pushed again and screamed. The nurse examined her again. "I see the head. Keep pushing." She grunted and heaved. As the baby emerged, relief flooded her body. It was over.

The nurse lifted the baby up for her to see. The baby suddenly transformed into a middle-aged woman. Sophia rubbed her eyes. The baby looked like her.

The dream had seemed so real, but there she was in this gaudy motel room in the middle of Nevada. She sat up in bed and glanced around the room. Ever since she had drunk the tea in the boutique, her dreams had been stranger than normal. The ringing of the phone jolted her.

"It's eight o'clock," the recording said.

She hung it up and flopped back down on the bed, snuggled deeply into the warm covers and allowed herself another hour of sleep. There was really no reason to get up this early. She didn't have an office to go to. She didn't have to make Brad's breakfast, or listen to his litany of things he wanted her to accomplish that day, and she didn't have to drag a sleeping teenager out of bed.

She was on the road by eleven. Las Vegas was four hours away. Once she arrived, she planned to call Cassandra and tell her she was going to spend the night and live it up. She hadn't been to Las Vegas in years, and she wanted to gamble at one of the new ritzy resorts on the Strip. Brad detested Las Vegas and its sinful ways, but she loved the pulsating energy. About ten years before, she and a girlfriend had flown down for a weekend of gambling, shopping, and dancing until early in the morning. When she returned and told him of her adventures, he called her a harlot.

"Well, screw you, Mr. Prissy," she said. "I am going to stay at an outrageously expensive hotel, gamble all I want, and send you the bill." She patted her purse where the American Express card still sat along with her MasterCard.

She fumbled with the radio dial. In her haste to leave, she had forgotten to pack some CDs. The only station that came in clear was NPR. She listened as the host and callers debated the state of the economy, education, and the latest political scandal. Politics had never interested her. In the seventies, she had registered as a Democrat in college because it was the anti-war party and never changed her affiliation. Brad was a staunch, stuffy Republican and active in the local chapter. The only reason she ever voted was to cancel his vote. She smiled as she remembered their heated arguments over the environment, taxes, and education.

Sophia turned off the radio and let her thoughts drift. She wasn't so sure about this goddess stuff. She had endured a strict Catholic upbringing, her mother had seen to that, and once she moved away she stopped attending church. She had had enough of the dry empty services where her only interest was in looking at what the other girls were wearing. Her first husband hadn't been interested in attending church, and Brad thought religion was for illiterate people, the same people who read fairy tales. Had she harmed her children? They had been one of the few families who hadn't attended services on Christmas or Easter. She didn't even know if Ben and Katie knew *The Lord's Prayer*.

Her thoughts drifted back to the woman in the boutique and her glowing magnificence. Marilyn was confident and beautiful, even though she had to be well into her sixties. *Was that diva power?* Because if it was, she wanted some.

She thought about Cassandra and her unusual ways. She had always been into alternative healing and thinking. Cassandra was the opposite of her mother, whose answer to every problem was to go to the mall and spend massive amounts of money on clothes she only wore once. She'd follow that with a trip to the spa to have her hair and nails done.

The two-lane road suddenly became four lanes. Sophia picked up her speed. She was approaching the Las Vegas Metro area. Traffic grew heavier. The air felt warmer, so she pulled over and put down the convertible top. The warm breeze caressed her hair as she pulled back on the highway.

She liked driving the little car. It was perfect. She chuckled as she imagined Brad's horror when he received the papers.

She slowed her speed. Traffic inched along the I15. Spying the Strip with its towering buildings spread out before her, she looked for Tropicana Avenue and wondered where she should stay. The Mirage, Caesar's Palace, Bellagio, Venetian, the Aladdin? The choices were endless. She decided to try the Bellagio. Several of her friends had stayed there and raved about the elegance and service. They mentioned it was expensive. Good, because she felt naughty.

Finding a parking space wasn't that easy, causing her to have to lug her suitcase across the acres of asphalt. Once inside the hotel, it took fifteen minutes to find the front desk. She stood in line and waited her turn. A young Asian man waved her over. "Do you have a reservation?" he asked.

"No. I was hoping you had a room for the night."

The man raised his thin eyebrows and cleared his throat. "Most of our guests have reservations. There are several conventions in town this week, and we are full."

Sophia reached for the American Express card and placed it on the counter. "I do hope you can help me. I was hoping to gamble in your fine establishment."

The man studied her. "I'll be right back. I have to check with my manager." He hurried to the back and whispered to an older gentleman dressed in a black tux. The man glanced at her, stroked his chin, then nodded. The clerk rushed back. "We have only one room left and it's usually reserved for one of our high rollers. You are in luck, because he cancelled this morning. It's five-hundred dollars for the night."

She gulped. Five hundred dollars! She had never paid that much for a room, but Brad was paying for it, so why not? "Put it on the card." She handed the card to the man and held her breath as he swiped it.

The man flipped the card over. "This card is in Brad Roberts' name. Who are you?"

She reached for the pen and signed the receipt. "Sophia Roberts. I'm authorized to sign. My husband will be joining me later. He's in a very important meeting. He's a lawyer. I'd like dinner reservations for two at your best restaurant. Let's say eight o'clock. And could you please send up a bottle of your finest champagne to our room?"

"It'll be taken care of, Mrs. Roberts. I'll send the bellman up with your luggage." He handed her the key and her credit card.

She took the elevator to the fifteenth floor and found her room at the end of the long hall. It was a large room decorated in soothing colors. There were blooming plants, a wet bar, a massive bed piled with thick pillows, and an entertainment center. A peek into the bathroom let out a long ahh from Sophia. The sunken tub looked inviting. After her luggage and the champagne were delivered, she filled the tub with water and bath salts, poured a glass of the bubbly liquid, peeled off her clothes, and stepped in. The warm water and champagne lulled her into a blissful state.

That evening she wandered through the designer shops located in the lobby. She purchased Katie a fancy tee-shirt, a shot glass for Ben that had the words *Las Vegas* printed on it, and a colorful scarf for Cassandra. She took the purchases up to her room, then headed back down to the casino and took a seat at one of the tables filled with Europeans. She placed her bet, then another one, and several more. Lady Luck was not on her side. After loosing a sizeable chunk of money, she excused herself and went to find the steakhouse. "Table for Mr. and Mrs. Roberts, please."

The attractive gentleman at the podium glanced up. "Ah, Mrs. Roberts." He looked around. "Where is Mr. Roberts?"

"He's not feeling well and went to bed."

"That's too bad. There is a nasty flu going around. Hopefully, you won't get it." He smiled. "Don't you look fabulous! Did you purchase that outfit in one of the hotel's boutiques?"

She smiled. "No. This I found in Reno."

The man's eyebrows rose. "I didn't know you could find couture in that cow town."

"Oh, Reno's grown," she said seductively. "We're not the country bumpkins of the north anymore."

The man blushed and led her through the crowded restaurant and over to a small table that overlooked the lighted swimming pool. "Can I bring you something from the bar?"

"A vodka martini, please."

"Very good. Thomas will be your server. Enjoy your meal." The man bowed slightly and walked to the bar.

Sophia leaned against the rich leather chair and surveyed the restaurant. Elegant men and women dressed in expensive clothes dined at candle-lit tables. Her martini was served. Chilled to perfection. She sipped the drink as she studied the menu. The prices were outrageous. So much the better. She chose grilled salmon, a Caesar salad, fresh vegetables, and tiny herbed potatoes. She didn't feel like eating much, but as she added up the amount in her mind, she smiled as she thought about Brad's reaction when he saw the bill. Her meal was served. She picked at the food, which was delicious, and sipped her third twelve-dollar martini. After ordering a decadent dessert, she nibbled a few bites, and left the rest. It was after eleven by the time she signed the bill.

"Excuse me, Madam," a male voice said, "but you are too beautiful to be dining alone. Would you care to join us for a drink?"

Sophia turned around. A group of men sat at a nearby table drinking and smoking cigars. "Thank you for the offer, but I have an early day tomorrow." She gracefully left the restaurant and hurried to her room. Her life certainly did not need to be more complicated than it already was, but the younger man with the blue pullover had been kind of cute.

"I'm leaving now," she told her aunt over the phone. "How long will it take me to drive to Sedona?"

"About five hours," Cassandra said, "but don't drive too fast. Savor the scenery. Has Brad contacted you yet? He's been calling here, and he's called your mom. Now she's all worried."

"He doesn't know where I am. He left a few messages on my cell, but I've deleted them. I don't want to talk to him."

"What did you do in Las Vegas, honey?"

"I'm at the Bellagio right now, had this outrageous dinner, ordered room service this morning, gambled lots of money, and put it all on his American Express."

Cassandra laughed. "That'll serve him right. How was it?"

"Expensive, elegant, and worth every penny. I'm going to leave now. I'll see you in a few hours." She hung up the phone and glanced around the room to see if she had gotten all her things. The phone rang as she was leaving. "Is this Mrs. Roberts?" the voice asked.

"Yes."

"A Mr. Roberts has contacted his credit card company and said you're not authorized to use this card. I'm afraid you're going to have to find another way to pay."

Sophia laughed. "That husband of mine. He can be quite the tease. Just send it back to the credit card company. They'll pay my charges. We're wonderful customers of American Express. Thank you." She hung up and left the room. The phone rang again, but she didn't answer. If they wanted to contact Brad, she had given the hotel all his information on the check-in form. It'll serve him right, she decided as she pressed the button for the elevator. She quickly slipped out of the hotel.

After stopping once in Boulder City to refuel and purchase a diet soda from the mini-mart, she bought a map and studied the route. It seemed fairly easy, but then she had difficulty with directions. She reached for her aunt's directions and placed them on the seat.

Several hours later she turned off the main road and followed 89A into Oak Creek Canyon. The dramatic red rocks loomed in front of her and she pulled off the road. She was stunned. The view was inspiring. Towering cliffs and pine trees gave way to red rock layers. The air sparkled. Something was stirring deeply inside her, something she had never felt before, and a sense of peace washed over her body.

Chapter 5

Sophia followed her scribbled directions, turned off the main road that ran through the center of town and into a well-maintained neighborhood. Most of the homes were set among tall pines, their red tile roofs catching the glimmer of the afternoon sun. She turned into the driveway of a small adobe-style home. As soon as she stepped out of the car, the front door burst open, and her aunt ran down the walkway, followed by a short, stocky man.

"You're here," Cassandra squealed, throwing her arms around Sophia's neck. "Let me take a good look at you." She pulled back. "You're awfully thin, but I can fix that."

Sophia hugged her aunt. "Thank you for having me. I don't want to be a nuisance." Cassandra looked magical dressed in a long flowing purple caftan. Her thick silver hair hung down her back and her face glowed.

"Nonsense," Cassandra said. "That's what family is for." She turned to the man, reaching for his hand. "This is Dave. My..." She hesitated. "Oh, what the hell. We're all adults. He's my lover."

Dave blushed and shook her hand. "It's nice to meet you. "I've heard so much about you. I'm sorry about your problems, but if there's anyone on this planet who can help you it's your aunt and her friends." His blue eyes twinkled. "I'm going to get home, dear. You two have much to catch up on and you don't need a man in the way. Don't forget you have a show this weekend, Cassandra."

"Don't worry. I'm all ready." Cassandra leaned over and kissed him passionately on the lips. "I'll see you tomorrow." He headed down the driveway, whistling a tune from an old musical.

"I was under the impression that you two lived together," Sophia said as she watched him head down the street.

Cassandra giggled like a schoolgirl. "Oh, he spends many nights here, sometimes too many for my liking. At this stage in my life, I relish my independence. Dave has a house two blocks over and we're together plenty. Believe me, I've played house with enough husbands and lovers for this lifetime. Let's get your things and we can have a nice visit." Cassandra reached into the backseat and lifted out one of Sophia's suitcases. "What do you have in here? Bricks?"

"Let me get that one. It's the heavier of the two. I didn't know what to bring." Sophia lifted the smaller bag out, handed it to her aunt, and picked up the heavier one. Brad had always nagged at her for over-packing, often unpacking some of her clothes. "When you get tired of me you can send me back," Sophia said with a grin.

She followed Cassandra into the house and set the bag down in the foyer, glancing into the living room off to the right. "This is charming." The walls were painted dusty pink. Light filtered through the slats of the plantation shutters. Indian artifacts were clustered on wooden tables, and colorful blankets hung from the walls. Tall green ferns stood in clay pots on the stone hearth.

"I love this house," Cassandra said. "The light is perfect for my work. I'll show you my studio later, but first let's get you settled."

Sophia followed Cassandra down a hall and into a bedroom adorned with a large brass bed, an antique hutch, and a writing desk. "I hope you will be comfortable," Cassandra said, plumping the pillows up on the bed and straightening the quilt.

"This is fabulous. Thank you." Sophia sat on the bed, suddenly feeling very tired.

Cassandra sat next to her. "Your soul is starving," she said, hugging her gently.

"Excuse me?"

Cassandra reached for one of her hands. "I see the energy around you. You need passion in your life, a reason to get up every morning. I see more and more women your age like this. They think that just because their children are grown, their marriage is over, or they've retired, they're finished with life. Nothing could be farther from the truth. A woman needs to dust herself off and reinvent her life. Your circumstances are your opportunities. You're just beginning the most exciting phase. And I know you don't want to hear this, but you're too thin. How can you enjoy life if you don't indulge in the physical pleasures that this plane of existence offers?"

Sophia turned her head, avoiding Cassandra's eyes. "I ate some salmon last night." She didn't want to tell her aunt that in the bottom of her suitcase was her trusty travel companion.

Cassandra sighed. "I remember what my sister did to you. You and Susan never received proper mothering. We're going to address that issue later, but first let's go into the kitchen and enjoy some tea." She hugged her. "I'm here to help you."

Sophia nodded, forcing away the tears that wanted to come. "I need to use the bathroom. I'll meet you in the kitchen."

"The bathroom is next door. There are clean towels and all kinds of bath goodies. Do you want to shower first?"

"I just need to freshen up, and I want to hang up my clothes." Sophia unzipped the suitcases, hung up her clothes, hid her scale under the bed, and went to the bathroom. As she walked into the kitchen, Cassandra turned around from the stove and handed her a cup of tea.

"This cup is like your mind. You can't take anything in right now because your mind is full. You must learn to edit out the distractions of the world, so you can concentrate on what's important to you. Sedona will help you accomplish that."

Sophia sipped the tea. Cassandra motioned for her to sit at the table, which overlooked a large patio filled with plants and budding flowers. Cassandra sat across from her and stared out the window. "Spring is almost here. A time for new beginnings. The light has returned. It is a good time to cultivate your creativity and heal the past."

She sipped the tea, all the while studying her aunt. "What's in this? It tastes rather exotic."

Cassandra smiled gently and sipped her own tea. "Something to take the edge off your nerves."

She laughed. "Do you think I need it?" She took another sip. "How long have you lived in Sedona now?"

Cassandra twirled a strand of long hair with her elegant fingers. "Hmm. It must be around twenty years. I was about your age when I arrived. I came here to heal after my third marriage failed." She laughed. "The bastard left me for his secretary. She was all of twenty-five. Can you imagine anything so dull? But then Phillip had no imagination. You should have seen him in bed. We always had sex on Sunday nights, and only on Sunday nights, and in the same position. He and that woman had two children. I'm sure they were conceived on Sunday nights in the military position. Now he's in his seventies raising teenagers. Serves him right. The universe always corrects wrong actions."

Sophia stared out the window and sighed. She was really no different from her mother and her aunt. All three of them had been left for younger women. "It's beautiful here. Why does this place attract so many artists?"

"It's the natural light and the energy from the vortexes. Plus the air is sparkling. No pollution up here." Cassandra paused. "Many people find some kind of connection with the red rocks and come here on a quest for renewal. Wait until you see the morning light on the rocks. It's spectacular."

"It was pretty impressive driving in. I remember the last time we stopped to see you. We were coming back from visiting Brad's parents in Phoenix and we spent the afternoon with you and that guy. Fred, I think his name was. Ben and Katie liked him. I wished we could have stayed longer, but Brad had to get home." She sighed. "He always had to get home. I've spent so many lonely weekends, and we cancelled so many vacations, because he was called into the office for some type of crisis."

Cassandra stretched her long legs. "Fred, hmm. He was a sculptor and fantastic in bed. He died several years ago of prostate cancer."

"I'm sorry to hear that. He seemed like a nice man."

Cassandra nodded. "He was, but it was his time to leave the planet. We'll meet again. I'm certain. But now I have Dave in my life, and he's sumptuous. He makes me feel so alive. He used to be an architect, but now he manages my career. He handles the show schedules and commissions pieces to galleries. I don't know what I'd do without him because I tend to not focus on things of that nature, but we're not here to talk about me. I want to talk about you."

Sophia finished her tea and set the mug down. "It's the same old tired story." She described running into Brad and Leslie in the Thai restaurant, and his decision to leave her because he was in love.

"I'm sorry, honey," Cassandra said softly. "I remember the hurt."

"You warned me about marrying him. I should have listened, but sometimes I'm too stubborn for my own good."

"That's true, but what's done is done. You and Brad produced two beautiful children. That's a blessing." Cassandra gazed out the window. "Sometimes I regret not having children, but it's too late now to worry about what might have been."

"I don't even see my children now. Ben's in Colorado and Katie's in Southern California. Ben is an attentive son. He calls weekly and sends me funny emails, but Katie and I still butt heads. She's her father's daughter and I can't do anything right."

"She'll come around, Sophia. I promise. It is written in the stars. You have to trust me on this."

"This is probably just payback from the way I treated my mother."

Cassandra smiled. "It's all part of the teenage angst. I remember your mother at odds with our mother."

"So what do I do now?" She studied her aunt. *Was there some kind of curriculum?*

"You need to empty your head for new growth. You were sent here to me and Sedona for a reason. It is time to release your divine nature. The divas will help you complete the necessary soul work for your wisdom years. Countless women have had to come to grips with their husbands leaving them for younger women, but they've kept their sense of humor, reconciled their aging body with society's harsh standards, and they've followed their own inner spiritual quest. They have been guided toward their innate creativity and have embraced new beginnings. After they have released their diva power, they have become ambassadors for the Goddess, teaching women who follow them how to be a real woman. I am here to teach you."

Sophia felt confused. She had never believed the magic of early childhood—fairies, invisible playmates, or guardian angels. "What if I don't believe in divas, the Goddess, or even God? What if I just want to stop the pain?"

Cassandra smiled gently. "You will stop hurting. I promise. All I ask is that you give the divas and the Goddess a chance. What do you have to lose?"

She leaned back in the chair and sighed. "Nothing. I just never believed in fairy tales or magic. Ask my mother."

Cassandra grinned. "I want you to turn around three times, click your heels together, and follow the yellow brick road. But there is one catch."

"I knew it. Do I have to kill the wicked witch of the west?"

"No," Cassandra said, her tone serious. "You need to listen carefully. The guidance and knowledge you seek will only come in solitude. When you quiet the mind, the divas will appear, and the lessons will unfold one at a time." She paused. "That's enough for one day. How about I show you around town and we get something to eat?" She stood and stretched her arms over her head. "I'm going to yoga tomorrow. Would you care to join me?"

Sophia's head buzzed. Goddesses, divas, diva power, and now yoga? She felt like she had tripped into some New Age novel. "I haven't practiced yoga since college."

"It's like riding a bike. Your body will remember. Why don't you grab a sweater? Nights are cool here."

Cassandra drove Sophia around the town of Sedona, pointing out places of interest. Sophia watched the red rocks darken and the shadows deepen as the sun lowered. Cassandra described the vortexes and the area's Native American heritage. "I have a map at the house. You need to hike each of the vortex trails. You can borrow my annual pass."

"Do I have to hike?" She felt so out of shape. She'd probably have a heart attack, die, and her body consumed by wild animals.

"That is where you'll meet some of the divas. Remember, I said they only appear when one is in solitude. They like to appear in nature or in your dreams."

"My dreams have been troubling lately," Sophia said.

"That's to be expected. It's part of the journey."

"Won't you hike with me in case I fall or something?" *Or if I meet a serial killer or a wild animal?*

Cassandra laughed. "I see your thoughts, Sophia. Don't worry. You will be protected. Besides, there are no serial killers in Sedona. The positive energy drives them away. The animals that live in the mountains won't hurt you." She smiled. "You will have to do this alone, but first you need to wait until your body acclimates." Cassandra pointed to two majestic buttes connected by a saddle. "That's Cathedral Rock. It's my favorite vortex and probably the most photographed vortex in Sedona."

"Isn't this the way I came in?" Sophia asked as she stared at the large red rock.

"You're right. I need to pick up something at the Village of Oak Creek." They continued along the two-lane highway. Cassandra pointed to another large formation. "That's Bell Rock."

She squinted. The sun was at that impossible angle. Bell Rock stood massively against the sky. "It does look like a bell."

"It was named for its shape. It's one of the easier hikes. You'll have fun exploring the area. The views from the top are spectacular." Cassandra pulled into a strip mall and parked in front of a health food store. "I'll be right back. I need to pick up a few herbs. Do you want anything?"

"I'm just going to close my eyes for a moment. I feel very tired."

"I'll be right back."

Sophia closed her eyes and the sounds of the highway lulled her mind. She felt her body drift away and discovered she was walking in a lush green meadow with sunlight streaming through the pines. A woman dressed in a flowing white gown appeared and smiled. "If one is controlled by another, she only has herself to blame because no one can be controlled unless she gives that power away. Sophia, you have been sent to the Red Rocks to release your personal power, but it is up to you to retrieve that power. It is a journey you must take alone."

The woman disappeared as quickly as she appeared. Sophia startled awake, opening her eyes. Had she been dreaming? Hallucinating? Maybe Cassandra was drugging her with that tea. What did that woman mean? She thought about it for a moment. She had always done what Brad told her to do. Oh, sometimes she protested silently, sometimes she was louder, but there was always a consequence when she didn't follow his demands. She shuddered.

Cassandra opened the car door and slid in. "Let's get something to eat. Do you like Mexican food?"

She started to tell her aunt about the woman, but decided to wait. "Mexican is fine."

The restaurant was small and cozy. A fire roared in the stone hearth. Sophia felt a wave of volcanic heat which started in her chest and spread throughout her body, and quickly removed her sweater. She sipped her water.

"Are you having a power surge?" Cassandra asked, her blue eyes twinkling in the dancing candlelight.

"Yes. Sometimes I can't control them, and I want to rip off all my clothes." She glanced around the crowded restaurant, noticing that it was filled with a younger crowd. "This would not be a good place."

Cassandra grinned. "I remember those days." She reached into her purse. "I picked these up for you when I was in the store. They'll help with your hot flashes." She handed Sophia a small brown bottle filled with tiny white pills.

"But I don't want to take anything. I've read the studies."

"Only if you take the pills made by drug companies. These are made by nature. Try them. I've been using them for years."

She opened the lid and shook one pill onto her palm. "Okay, but only because I don't want to drip in public." She swallowed the pill with a sip of water. "I can't predict these hot flashes. I can go for days without one. Then I'll break out in a sweat in a business meeting or a social event."

"These will help. Now let's eat. I'm famished." Cassandra picked up the menu.

Sophia reached for one as well and examined her choices. Most of the entrees were filled with fat. The words of her mother echoed. "I'll just have a salad."

Cassandra sipped her water, studying Sophia over the rim of the glass. "I'm not going to argue with you today. I'm hungry. Have whatever you want."

Sophia ordered a dinner salad and a cup of tortilla soup. She picked at her meal while Cassandra dug into a chicken tostado filled with tomatoes, shredded lettuce, guacamole, sour cream, cheese, and beans. She stared at her aunt as she ate with gusto and wished that she could do the same, but the demons haunted her every time she thought about food. By the time they were finished and the check taken care of, Sophia was exhausted. She allowed Cassandra to lead her to the car and she slept on the way back. Once at the house, Cassandra eased her into bed and covered her with blankets. "I'll be in my studio in the morning. Yoga's at eleven."

Chapter 6

Sophia dreamt she was trekking through the Himalayas dressed as a pilgrim and carrying a walking stick. She hiked the steep path and stood at a tall iron gate. A posted sign read: *All who enter must shed their past.* Her walking stick suddenly transformed into a gleaming silver sword, and she swung it through the air.

She awoke and opened her eyes. Sunlight streamed through the curtains. After giving herself a good stretch in the bed, she reflected on the dream and her legs became entangled in the cotton sheets. *Shed the past? How do I do that?* The past was part of her, wrapped tightly in her muscles and bones. She threw on a bathrobe and headed toward the studio, knowing her aunt would be at work.

The large room she entered had tall windows facing south. Classical music played softly and chimes sang. Vivid colors covered every wall. Art work was scattered throughout the studio: paintings, sculptures, pottery. Thick colorful rugs were spread on the tile floor. Several fountains trickled water, and green plants stretched toward the abundant light. In the midst of this splendor sat Cassandra, working at the pottery wheel, her hands immersed in thick dark clay. Sophia saw shelves of clay pots at every stage of completion. There was a large wooden easel with an oil painting in progress. "Good morning," she said. "This is an awesome room."

Cassandra turned around, took her foot off the pedal, and grinned. "Well, good morning, sleepyhead. I was just about to wake you. Yoga's in an hour." She stood, wiped her hands on her denim apron, and went to a small hot plate with a kettle on top. She poured a cup of tea. "Drink this, please."

Sophia wrinkled her nose. "Do you have any coffee?"

"I haven't had coffee in the house in years. Tea is healthier." Cassandra smiled. "If you want, we can pick up some at the market after yoga."

"I'm afraid I'm addicted to coffee. I drink three cups in the morning just to feel normal, then I drink diet cola throughout the day." She sipped the tea. "What kind of tea is this?"

"It's my special blend designed to stir the creative juices in your soul."

Sophia took the tea and went to the wicker rocker and sat. "I could definitely create some art in your studio. The light and energy are fantastic."

"Please do. I usually work in the morning, and I need to be alone, but after that the studio's all yours. Did you know that creativity is our original spark, the unique and individual mark that each woman makes upon the world? Creativity is bestowed on us by the Goddess?"

Sophia continued sipping her tea. "If you say so." It was too early in the morning for fairy tales.

"Let me show you some of the things I plan on placing in the show this weekend. I'd like your opinion." Cassandra walked over to a shelf filled with Raku pottery and picked up a bowl. "This is my new collection. I'm calling it *Vision of the Red Rocks*. What do you think?"

Sophia examined the pottery. "They're spectacular. I love the deep colors. I noticed the easel. When did you start oil painting?"

"About six years ago. This is a dramatic area to paint with its monumental geology. I've taken several classes and I'm developing as a painter. I've sold quite a few. One of the interesting things about Sedona is that there are more art galleries than citizens. Most of the tourists who visit want to take home a piece of art." She pointed to a large oil painting of a cluster of red rocks. "Several of my paintings are lithographs. People can purchase a picture at a fraction of the original cost and still enjoy the painting." She pointed to another painting. "This is the Chapel of the Holy Cross. It's one of my favorite places in Sedona. If you visit on a day when there are not too many visitors, you can feel the intense energy of the church. It's magical. I plan to take you there."

Catholic guilt unleashed from Sophia's cells and flooded her bloodstream. "I'm not into churches."

Cassandra smiled gently. "It's not what you think, Sophia. One needs to have an open mind. And speaking of open minds, we're off to yoga shortly. Slip into comfortable clothes. I'll meet you outside in fifteen minutes."

Sophia went back to her room, threw the comforter over the sheets, and searched for something to wear. She unearthed a pair of black leggings and a gray tee shirt in the bottom of her suitcase and tied a sweatshirt loosely around her waist. What was Cassandra dragging her into? Yoga was for hippies.

Sophia's graduating high school class had been at the end of that turbulent era. Having attended Catholic school, there was never a discussion with her mother of whether to wear peace signs, headbands, or bell-bottom jeans to school. She was forced to look like a lady and the mere remembrance of the unbecoming dark uniforms she had been forced to wear caused her to grimace. She had been heavy in high school, and she always thought the stupid uniform made her look like a refrigerator. She remembered the nuns, dressed in their starched penguin suits, had spread guilt on her soul as thick as peanut butter.

"Sophia, "Cassandra yelled. "We're going to be late."

"Coming," she yelled back while running a brush quickly through her short blond hair, noticing several new patches of gray and wondering when she had last had her hair colored.

Cassandra waited at the front door with two mats and two bottles of water. "Do you mind driving? I can't seem to find my keys?"

"Sure. Just tell me where to go." Sophia reached into her purse for her keys and the two women slid into the VW bug. With the exception of one woman digging in her garden, the street was quiet. Cassandra dictated directions while Sophia struggled to follow.

"This car suits you," Cassandra said. Her long hair fluttered in the wind. "Turn in there." She pointed to a small wooden building.

Sophia pulled into the crowded parking lot. "I like it. I traded in the Volvo the day I left." She giggled.

"Now you're sounding like a woman who's releasing her diva power. Good job."

She followed Cassandra into a large room with gleaming hardwood floors. Students were lying on their mats stretching their legs and backs. The class faced the mirrored wall. Cassandra led her to an open spot and spread out their mats. A tall, balding man walked to the front of the room and stood with his hands clasped. "We're just in time," Cassandra whispered. "This teacher can be intense, and he's very punctual."

"Please stand," the man said. He waited as the class stood. "Breathe in and out from your nose only," he commanded. "Focus on the breath. It will take you to your final destination. If thoughts come into your mind, let them go. Do not attach to them. Let's start with Sun Salutation."

Sophia struggled to follow along, but her muscles screamed from inactivity. When was the last time she stretched? She couldn't even touch her toes, while Cassandra was graceful and fluid in her movements. The teacher came over and helped Sophia with a few postures. "Don't give up," he said softly. "Yoga takes patience. Don't judge yourself with your neighbors. You're only in competition with yourself. This is yoga practice, not yoga perfect. Use the breath to open up the tight areas of your body and don't attach to your thoughts."

She nodded. Did he realize how difficult this was for her? She had never been very graceful. Her dance teacher had told her mother that dancing was not in her blood and suggested baseball. That horrified her mother because she was determined that both her girls would learn dance. The yoga teacher pressed on her back when she was bent over in Downward Dog, and she felt her muscles scream. She whimpered. He smiled and walked over to another student.

Finally, the class was over and they lay in corpse position. She closed her eyes. This was the one position she could do correctly. She struggled to concentrate on her breathing, but it was difficult. Thoughts danced across her mind. How was she going to support herself? What about health insurance? Brad carried their insurance. Who was going to hire a fifty-year-old woman who had stayed home to raise her children, then attempted a career in real estate, which she sucked at? Breathe, Sophia, she reminded herself. Let it go. But the concerns still tromped through her mind. After a few minutes, the lights turned on. "You may open your eyes," the instructor said. "Class is over. Thank you for coming. Namaste."

Cassandra leaned over and reached for Sophia's arm. "You did great. Are you ready to go?"

Sophia opened her eyes, groaned, stood, leaned backwards, and stretched. She knew she was going to be sore. She rolled up her mat and followed Cassandra out of the room.

"I've got to pick up a few things at the market," Cassandra said. "I'll buy you a sandwich."

She handed Cassandra her car keys. "Could you drive? I'm wasted." A few minutes later, they pulled into the parking lot of the largest health food store Sophia had ever seen. "I thought you said we were going to a grocery store."

Cassandra turned off the engine and grinned. "I believe I said market. Grocery stores are so pedestrian."

Sophia grabbed her purse and followed her aunt into the store, her body feeling stiff and sore. She grabbed a basket and wandered the crowded aisles, her muscles aching, and studied her choices. She hated to admit it, but the food looked healthier than it did in the grocery store by her house she frequented. Perhaps Cassandra's food choices were another reason she vibrated with energy. She didn't want to burden her aunt with having to pay to feed her, so she chose several juices, a carton of yogurt, organic tomatoes and lettuce, free-range chicken, whatever that meant, wild rice, sprouted whole wheat bread, several cheeses, and coffee. She was going to make herself a strong cup when she got back to Cassandra's

"What are you doing?" Cassandra asked.

Sophia turned around and saw her aunt's cart brimming with food. "I'm going to contribute. I can cook. Tonight I'll make chicken."

"That would be wonderful. I've never been excited over cooking. Your mother got that gene. Our mother, or rather her housekeeper, was a fabulous cook. Your mother used to spend hours in the kitchen with Claire learning her secrets. I do try to eat healthy. It costs more, but I save on doctor's visits. I haven't been to a traditional doctor in over ten years."

"Don't you get a physical and a mammogram yearly?" Her own health insurance worries nagged. She saw her name scratched out on the family's insurance card, and Leslie's neatly typed in.

Cassandra shook her head. "There are alternative approaches I utilize. Are you ready to check out?"

Sophia followed Cassandra to the checkout line and waited her turn. When the cashier rang up her purchases, she handed the American Express card. *Why not keeping using it?* The girl swiped it, pursed her lips, then handed the card back to her. "The card's no longer valid. How are you going to pay for this?"

She blushed. The gig was up. He really had cancelled it. "Here, try this," she said, handing her the MasterCard. She felt a sigh of relief when that card was accepted. How was she going to pay that bill? That was the only card she had in her own name, and she had always been responsible for its bill. She had gone on line and requested the card when she received her first paycheck from the real estate firm. "Brad cancelled the card," she told her aunt as she put her bag in the back seat.

"Well, you had a good run for awhile, didn't you? Left him with some big bills." Cassandra started the car and they headed home.

Sophia thought for a moment, calculating the damage she had done. Then she giggled. "Well, I spent almost two thousand at the boutique, a hundred or so in Tonopah, and a couple of grand in Vegas."

"I think he got what he deserved," Cassandra said, pulling into the driveway. "Why don't we eat our sandwiches in the garden after we put the groceries away? It's lovely out there this time of day."

Sophia stretched her legs in the warm sun and bit into the sandwich. It was filled with avocado, sprouts, sliced tomatoes, peppers, and cheese. She quickly counted the calories, wondering if she should remove the avocado, but she felt Cassandra's gaze and took another bite. "I feel healthier already," she said. "For lunch usually I pop a frozen meal into the microwave, or I skip it all together." She didn't want to tell her aunt that her frozen meals often had less than three hundred calories. There had to be three hundred calories in one bite of this sandwich.

Cassandra sipped her mineral water. "Frozen food is full of preservatives. I think it would be wise to detoxify your body before you start your journey." Her tone grew serious. "You might want to gain a few pounds."

Knowing where the conversation was headed and not wanting to get into it, she decided to ignore that comment. "When am I supposed to start this journey?"

"First I think we need to discuss your eating disorder."

"I don't have an eating disorder."

"Then what do you call it?" Cassandra asked softly. "You barely eat enough to keep a bird alive. I remember what my sister did to you. I've never forgiven her. Sophia, please listen. Eating disorders are diseases of the feminine soul. You need to tend your wound before you start this journey."

Sophia's head swam with memories of her adolescence. She had tried to blot out that horrible period in her life, but the albatross of her mother's words still hung around her neck like a weighted necklace: "You're fat and unacceptable. No sorority is going to accept you. No man is ever going to marry you with cottage-cheese thighs. We're disgusted. No daughter of ours is going to look the way you do. It shows a lack of self-discipline. You're going to have to take off that weight now. You're an embarrassment. What did we do wrong? I lie awake at night and worry. Your father and I have decided that you are going on a diet right now. And you're going to start exercising everyday. Rain or shine." Her mother stood in the kitchen of their home speaking the words that haunted her for years.

"Sophia," Cassandra said gently, "are you still with me?"

She felt the hot tears flood her eyes and nodded. "God, it seems like yesterday. I can still see her standing in the kitchen, with her hands perched on her skinny hips, wagging her finger at me. What really hurts is that my father just stood by the counter and didn't say a word. It's been over thirty years and it feels like yesterday."

Cassandra wrapped her arms around her. "I'm so sorry, honey. Image was always very important to my sister. I know she hurt you and your sister Susan terribly."

Sophia reached into her pocket and found a tissue and blew her nose. "You should see Susan now. I'm so proud of her. She quit throwing up. She's gained weight, and she and her husband are happy living on the farm in upstate Vermont. She refuses to come home and visit. I probably need to call her and tell her about things."

"You should," Cassandra said. "When was the last time you saw your mother?"

"Katie and I went down to USC last spring to check out the campus. We spent an afternoon with her. That was all I could take." Sophia laughed. "It's funny, but now I'm too thin. She doesn't like my hair. I need a perm or some type of thickening hair gel." She paused. "What did I ever do to her?"

"Nothing, Sophia. You're perfect the way you are. It's her, not you. I saw her several months ago. Dave and I flew to Laguna Beach because I had several pieces in a gallery, and she happened to be there for the weekend. She's still rail thin, tanned, and smokes a pack of cigarettes a day. I'm surprised she hasn't died from skin or lung cancer."

"God, she was relentless when I was growing up." Sophia said. "She lectured me constantly about my weight and compared me to Susan. 'Look how trim Susan is. Why can't you look like her?' I tried. I really did, but it wouldn't last long. At the time, I didn't know Susan's secret. I tried throwing up once, but..." She grimaced. "It was tough living in Southern California in the late sixties and early seventies. If you didn't look like the models on the covers of the magazines, you never got a prom date. The funny thing is I don't think it's changed. I watch Katie and her friends. The pressure society puts on young girls. It's amazing more of them don't snap."

Sophia stared at her aunt and started to cry softly. "I tried, Cassandra. I tried so hard to lose the weight she wanted. I followed the grapefruit diet, the protein diet, and every other diet I found in the magazines. I fasted and drank nothing but carrot juice, but that scale refused to budge. Then one day, magically the weight started to slide off. Perhaps my metabolism changed. I don't know, but I lost twenty pounds quickly."

"I remember." Cassandra said softly. "You quit eating."

"But after I started losing weight, there were always other issues according to Mother. My grades, my hair, my makeup. I don't understand. Why can't she love me?"

"Because she doesn't love herself. If you don't love yourself, then you can't transfer that love to another person."

Sophia blew her nose into her napkin. "I feel like a complete failure."

"I can see you're hurting. I think we've discussed this subject enough for one day. I only want to help you heal. Eat what you can." Cassandra smiled warmly. "Why don't you go into the studio this afternoon and play?"

She set her sandwich down. She was done eating. "I'd like that."

Sophia spent the afternoon in the light-filled studio, staring at the tubes of paint—burnt sienna, cadmium red, yellow ochre—and remembering the thrill of making art. She mixed several colors. Slowly and deliberately she picked up the brush, wetted the paper, dipped the brush into the mixture of paint, and spread it on the paper. It felt marvelous. She painted an abstract of the view from the window, then tried her hand at pottery. She felt frustrated. It didn't matter how she constructed the bowl, it fell apart when she put it on the wheel. She scooped up the clay and put it back into the bucket. She'd go back to watercolors. That was safer.

By the end of the afternoon, she was exhausted. She took a quick shower and settled in for a long nap. Cassandra had left her a note saying she and Dave were hiking. She turned on her cell phone to check for messages. Katie had called, asking for money. She laughed. There was no money to give her now. Ben called to check on her. Her mother called and told her to grow up and go back home, get a good lawyer, and sue him for everything he's worth. The last message was from Brad.

"I'm sure you know by now I cancelled the American Express. How could you spend all that money? You know we don't have that kind of money right now. I realize I've hurt you, and I'm sorry. I didn't purposely fall in love with Leslie. It just happened. You have to believe me. Please come home, so we can sort out our situation. You're acting childish by not answering your phone. And what's with the new car? Sophia, you cannot keep running up expenses if we're going to dissolve this marriage."

How dare him! She dialed his office, crossing her fingers that she would get voice mail, and she did. "You're going to have to come down here if you want to talk," she said. "And for the record, Counselor, I'm not the one acting childish. You're the one sleeping with a girl young enough to be your daughter. I saw the bank book. How much of our money have you spent on her?"

Chapter 7

On a bright sunny afternoon, while in the studio, Cassandra was giving Sophia a lesson on the pottery wheel. She was having a hard time and wiped her clay-stained hands on her jeans. "I'm never going to get this. I'm too old to start pottery."

"Nonsense. You're never too old." Cassandra's tone grew serious. "Let me tell you a secret about aging. The key to staying young is to always be a beginner at something. Learn new things, become engaged in life, then you'll never become boring or old."

Sophia stared at her aunt. The idea seemed enormous. She was fifty, too old to start a career. Or was she? She had read about women going back to school in their fifties and sixties and becoming doctors and lawyers. "I guess you're right. I am scared. I don't know what to do with my life."

Cassandra tilted her head. The afternoon sun bathed her face and she radiated energy. Sophia's breathing slowed as Cassandra's eyes drew her into her energy field and she reached for her hand. "Explore whatever has energy for you. Do you want to paint, throw clay, write, create a garden? Do you want to become a . . . gourmet chef?" She laughed. "Okay," Cassandra said. "Perhaps not that, but the opportunities are endless. The universe is a marvelous place and the Goddess is loving and kind. She only wants the best for us, so she has sprinkled each of us with stardust. All you have to do is activate that energy."

Sophia chuckled. "There you go with that fairy tale stuff. I don't think I've heard this many fairy tales since I read them to the kids."

Cassandra grinned. "The language of fairy tales speaks to the soul. Perhaps life is a fairy tale, and we're all sleeping until we awaken. Maybe you're really Sleeping Beauty, and you're finally waking up to your life at fifty."

"If I remember the story correctly, Sleeping Beauty was awakened by a handsome prince. My prince left me for another woman."

"Then he really wasn't your prince, was he?" Cassandra asked softly. "All you have to do is ask and you will receive. It's as simple as that."

Sophia thought about all the things she had asked for that had never come true. She had really wanted a puppy when she was little, but her mother, a constant clean freak, refused. She wanted Tim O'Brien to ask her to the prom, but he took Candy Lewis. She had prayed for more children after Katie, but her ovaries refused. And she had prayed that Brad would come to his senses and leave Leslie, because she was scared to be alone. Lately, she prayed that she'd win the lottery because then she wouldn't need to worry about money. "I've asked for many things and they've never come true," she finally said.

"The universe will grant requests if they're in your best interest. Winning the lottery usually isn't in a person's best interest. If one wants money, she needs to exchange the necessary energy to receive it."

Sophia stared at her aunt. *Was she a mind-reader?* "How did you know I wanted to win the lottery?"

Cassandra giggled. "I read your energy. You think by winning a chunk of money you'll solve all your problems with a dash of the pen. People with money have just as many problems as those without. You need to find your passion and create money from that passion. Then your life will be exciting and fulfilling."

She bit her lip. She hated to admit it, but Cassandra made sense. And Brad thought she was wacky? "There is something I've always wanted to do," she said in a small, quiet voice.

"What is that?"

Sophia hesitated a bit, wondering that if she spoke her dream out loud she'd jinx it. She had never told another soul, only the scribbled pages of her journal. "I want to write and illustrate children's books. All the years I spent reading to Ben and Katie, along with the years of volunteering in the school library, gave me a good idea of what kids like. I want to write books that make then laugh and forget their problems. Today's world is too complex for children."

Cassandra smiled. "I think that would be wonderful. Children need positive images. The media is taking away their childhood. Too many parents rely on the digital nanny and because of this many homes are shattered."

"I don't even know where to start."

"Art takes discipline. You need to make time for it every day, not just when the muse strikes. I have something for you. I'll be right back. Cassandra hurried out of the room and returned with a stack of art supplies. "I had fun at the art store the other day." She placed them on Sophia's lap. "This is your license to explore the world, to write your stories, and heal your soul." She leaned over and kissed her on the cheek.

Sophia stared at the sketch pad, water colors, drawing pencils, and colored pencils. "I don't know what to say. No one's ever treated me this kindly. Thank you."

"It was my pleasure. Just remember, we are all artists. Some of us just need encouragement."

Hot tears filled Sophia's eyes. "Did I tell you what Brad said about my paintings?" Cassandra shook her head. "He said they were primitive, and the only place I could hang them was in the garage where guests wouldn't be subjected to them."

"Ouch! That must have hurt." Cassandra stood and held out her hand. "It's time for you to visit my serenity room. It's my sacred place where wonders occur. Follow me."

Sophia set her things down, took off her apron, and followed Cassandra to the back of the house where she was ushered into a small room. There were statues of women on an altar and shelves packed with books. She walked over and ran her hand over the subjects: Zen, Hindu, Buddhism for Beginners, Celtic, and Wicca. Crystals dangled from the ceiling catching the afternoon sun and a tabby-colored cat slept in a white wicker chair in the corner. Cassandra came behind her and stroked the cat's shiny fur. "This is Dinah. She found me several years ago. She stays in this room, that's why you haven't met her. I think she's about fifteen or sixteen years old."

Cassandra smiled gently at Sophia. "The universe has guided you here to release the power you have kept locked up inside of you. You have the makings of an artist. I see it in your aura, but first you need to tend to your soul." She closed the shades, lit the candles and incense on the altar, and motioned Sophia to sit on one of the plump floor cushions facing the altar. Cassandra then poured a glass of water from a crystal pitcher. "When I first awake in the mornings, I come here, even before the studio. It centers me before I work." She handed Sophia the glass. "Drink this water and ask it to purify your thoughts. I'm going to perform a ceremony to awaken your creativity."

Cassandra picked up a large drum and beat it strongly with her hand, chanting unfamiliar words. Sophia closed her eyes, struggling to keep her mind in the room. It wanted to wander. After several minutes, she found herself concentrating to the sound of the beat, feeling something deep inside her stir, as if she really was Sleeping Beauty and awakening from a long sleep.

"Inhale, exhale," Cassandra said softly. "Open your eyes and focus on the flames. Release all self-criticism and other people's voices from your mind."

Sophia followed the instructions. Time passed. She couldn't tell you how much time, and then the drumming stopped. Cassandra placed an object in her hand. "I give you this crystal. Hold it tightly and feel its power awaken your dormant originality. Creativity is the part of your soul that needs to express itself."

Sophia glanced down at her hand. A small, smooth lavender stone rested in her palm. She clutched it tightly, feeling the energy of the room shift. The flames shot to the ceiling. She focused on her breath: inhale, exhale. Cassandra picked up the drum, beating it loudly and chanting words. Time expanded. Sophia felt her soul leave her earthly body and soar through the sky. She journeyed into the star-filled heavens where the beams of colored light connected to various parts of the galaxy. The sun exploded into a rainbow of whirling light. She discovered that she was in the grand court of a gleaming palace with exquisitely polished marble floors. Water fountains musically jingled and the sweet smell of jasmine filled the air. A swirling ball of light approached and slowly took form. The most beautiful woman she had ever seen stood before her dressed in a flowing white gown and holding a golden wand. She knew she was in the presence of a higher power.

"I am waiting for you, Sophia," the beautiful woman said. "Do not be afraid. I am here to help you. Follow the divas' directions, complete the tasks, and I will meet you when you are ready. Know that I am with you always." The beautiful woman waved her wand, suddenly transforming into a ball of light, and soared towards the heavens.

Sophia was jolted back into her body. She opened her eyes and stared at her aunt. "I just met the most beautiful woman. I don't know who she is, but I think she's really important."

Cassandra grinned. "All will be revealed in good time. It is part of the journey. Anytime you feel confused, and you feel that you have lost touch with your essence, find a place you can be alone. Take out your crystal, pour a glass of pure water, and light a candle. Meditate by concentrating on the flame and know you are always protected. Then you can pick yourself up, dust off the debris of being human, and proceed."

* * *

"How was yoga?" Dave asked as Sophia entered the kitchen. He stood at the stove stirring a pot. "It's vegetable stew." He grinned widely.

She sat at the table. "I love to see a man working in the kitchen. The only time Brad ever came in the kitchen was to bark orders at me." She stretched her legs. "I'm so sore. That yoga stuff is really difficult. The stew smells great. I know you want to hear this. I am really hungry. I promise I'll eat. Cassandra made me take two yoga classes today and hike for an hour. I can't keep up with her. When are you coming to yoga?" she teased, with a slight lift of an eyebrow and a faint tilt of her head.

"When Cassandra takes judo lessons. We have a deal," Dave said, "but most likely that will be in the next lifetime."

Cassandra entered the kitchen, throwing her purse on the counter. "I like the fluidity and peacefulness of yoga." She kissed Dave on the cheek. "The stew smells great. Do I ever tell you how grateful I am for having you in my life?"

Dave stirred the pot with a wooden spoon. "I think I hear that everyday, but I could hear it more. I have a fragile male ego."

"I think you're wonderful," Cassandra said, nuzzling his neck.

"I have to go to Phoenix tomorrow for a meeting," Dave said. "Do you want to come?"

"That'll work out. There are a few things I need to do there. It might be good for Sophia to have the house to herself."

"Is she ready for the gatekeeper?" Dave asked.

"Not yet. She has an appointment with Ruby in two days, and then she'll decide if she's ready," Cassandra said.

"Who's Ruby? Why is it her decision if I'm ready or not?" Sophia paused. "Ready or not for what?"

"Ruby's a shaman who lives in the mountains. She's the gatekeeper of the journey. If she thinks you're ready, she'll give you her blessing." Cassandra turned toward Dave. "I'm hungry. Can we eat now?"

Cassandra and Dave left early the following morning for Phoenix. Cassandra handed a list to Sophia. "These are things I want you to do today. Number one is very important. No talking. A day of silence is good for the soul. You'll be amazed at how much energy you'll have at the end of the day." Sophia started to open her mouth, wondering how she was going to keep quiet all day, but Cassandra gently put her hand over her mouth. "Silence starts now. And don't forget your yoga class and the hike I've marked."

Sophia watched them drive way and wondered how she was going to keep quiet for twelve hours. In school she had been admonished for talking. She shivered as she remembered the horror of marching to the front of the class and having to place her hands out to receive the sting of the nun's wooden ruler. In high school, she had spent afternoons chatting on the phone with her friends. Even today, when there was no one to talk to, she often talked to herself.

It was a struggle, but she managed to spend the day in silence. She nodded to her classmates in yoga, smiled when she encountered other hikers on the trail, and spent the afternoon hours creating a dramatic watercolor of the Verde Valley in the studio. By the time Dave and Cassandra returned, she felt like she glowed. "Angel hair pasta with eggplant sauce," she said as she served dinner. "And I'll have you know these are the first words I've spoken all day."

Cassandra took a bite, twirling the pasta on her fork. "This is delicious." She winked at Dave. "We should leave you alone more often."

A strong north wind blew, rattling the windows and shaking the house. Sophia struggled with sleep—tossing and turning, but finally falling asleep after counting millions of proverbial sheep. When she awoke the following morning and peered through the curtains, she saw thick dark clouds hovering over the red rocks. The ground was wet and the temperature felt as if it had dropped twenty degrees. She shivered, reached for her robe, and padded out to the kitchen. Cassandra and Dave sat at the table drinking tea and reading the newspaper. "What happened to the weather?" she asked, reaching for a mug. She was growing accustomed to the strange tastes of Cassandra's exotic tea blends.

"A storm is approaching," Dave said. "Weather changes quickly here. You'll want to make sure you dress warm today."

Sophia sat at the table and took the cup of steaming tea from her aunt. She wrinkled her nose as she took a sip. "This is different. I haven't had this before." She stared at her aunt. Something was up. "Where are we going today?"

Cassandra glanced up from the paper, her glasses sitting on the end of her nose, and smiled. "Ruby's expecting you this afternoon. After yoga. I hope you brought some warm clothes."

* * *

Sophia turned off the highway and onto a dirt road, then stopped at a driveway. "This is it?"

"Turn down the driveway. Her house is at the end," Cassandra said.

Driving carefully, so as not to damage her new car, Sophia eased down the driveway. They had taken her car because Cassandra's car had blown a fuel pump and was in the garage. She parked outside a small adobe bungalow and they got out. Cassandra knocked on the door. "Come in," a woman yelled. "I'm in the kitchen."

The wooden door yawned as they entered the tiny house. Several ceiling fans whirled overhead. A fire roared in the fireplace and a black cat slept on the divan not too far from an old Spaniel sprawled across the bare wooden floors. The dog's tail thumped as Sophia leaned over and patted its fur. A diminutive woman with thick gray braids that hung down her back entered the room. "It's good to see you, Cassandra," the woman said grinning. The woman turned to Sophia. "I am Ruby, the gatekeeper of the journey. You must be Sophia."

With a warm nod, Sophia shook the woman's outstretched hand. "Yes, I am. It's nice to meet you."

Ruby wiped her hands on her apron, her broad flat face beamed as she hugged her. "I see the energy around you. It is time. I've made a special tea for the occasion. Please sit by the fire and I'll be right back." She hurried to the kitchen and returned with a tray. She handed Sophia a steaming mug. "This is what you need."

More tea, she thought as she took the mug and sipped the tea. It tasted strange, but then she had drunk nothing but exotic teas since she arrived. She followed Ruby over to the couch.

"I need to ask you a personal question," Ruby asked.

Sophia stared at the strange-looking woman. "Go ahead."

"Do you keep the blood?"

Sophia blushed. She wasn't accustomed to discussing her bodily functions with strangers. "Do you mean have I gone through the change?"

Ruby nodded.

Feeling a bit stunned and somewhat embarrassed, Sophia leaned into the cushions and thought. "I can't remember my last period. Perhaps it was a year ago. I was experiencing hot flashes until I started following Cassandra's advice." She glanced at her aunt. "Now they're gone."

Cassandra beamed. "I told you they would leave if you followed my recommendations."

"You always bring me the most promising students," Ruby told Cassandra. She reached into her pocket and handed Sophia a colored beaded bracelet with a tiny gold key dangling at the end. "This is for you. You need to wear this on your journey."

Sophia took the bracelet from Ruby. The golden key shimmered in the light. She slipped the bracelet over her wrist. It reminded her of a bracelet Katie had made one summer while away at camp.

"This bracelet is worn by all apprentices," Ruby said. "I want you to listen carefully to what I have to say, Sophia. You are about to embark on a journey designed to release your divine diva. Once upon a time, many years ago, east of the sun and west of the moon, your spirit was exhaled by the Mother of all and set forth to begin its journey to enlightenment. Over the eons of time, women have lost their way because they had not listened to their hearts and have become entangled in their heads. During the journey, you will meet divas who will present you with tasks. You will complete the tasks and follow the ancient path of all women back to your source." Her tone grew serious. "Many women refuse the tasks. They don't want to do the necessary work. They complain that it is too hard, yet they complain about the status of their own lives. I will not lie to you. The work is hard, but it is crucial to the process. Every woman's journey is unique. Please listen carefully, because this is important."

Sophia put her tea down and stared at the old woman.

Ruby continued. "If at midlife, a woman has spent a lifetime developing the physical and neglecting the spiritual, one day she will look in the mirror and discover that her exterior has faded and her interior is vacant. This is sad and I don't understand it. In my culture, a woman anticipates her wisdom years. It is the time when she is revered by the tribe. Her words are like jewels, and she becomes the wise woman. She helps others with their struggles." She shook her head. "Women in your society are only concerned with smoother skin, thinner thighs, and sparkling diamonds. Material possessions and tight skin won't help you when you leave this plane of existence."

Sophia was finally beginning to understand. "I read this article in the paper about a best-selling author who went in for some cosmetic surgery to tighten her chin. I guess someone told her that her chin was sagging. She died unexpectedly from complications, and she was only fifty-two. What makes this so sad is that her body of work dealt with men leaving women for younger models. I think she referred to a second wife as a trophy wife."

"I read that article, too," Cassandra said. "It is a tragedy."

Ruby nodded. "This type of thinking is prevalent in your society. Women over fifty are not valued."

"How do I go forward?" Sophia asked, this time with complete sincerity.

"Tomorrow you will receive your first assignment. It is a task chosen specifically for you, but you need to be patient and listen carefully. All will be revealed in good time."

"Patience is hard for me."

"Patience is a very important trait to master," Ruby said. She leaned over and lightly stroked Sophia's cheek. "A diva honors the path of every soul and allows them to explore themselves without judgment. A diva recognizes that all spiritual paths are valid. She finds her authentic voice and releases her power. You are ready. I give you my blessing. You now wear the bracelet. You will be protected."

"From what? Wild animals?"

Ruby and Cassandra giggled. "The animals will be your guides to many of the divas," Ruby explained.

Sophia gulped. "Animals!"

"Don't worry. You will be protected. Come with me out to the sweat lodge. You need to cleanse your body, mind, and spirit before you embark on this journey. Cassandra, do you want to join us?"

Cassandra stood. "I always need a good sweat." She winked at Sophia. "You're going to like this."

She wasn't so sure about that as she followed the women into the lodge, which was really just heavy woolen blankets and plastic tarps placed over thick branches. She had never liked the heat. It made her dizzy. She sat on the cool earth next to Cassandra. "I'm going to bring in some of the hot rocks," Ruby said. "I'll be right back."

Sophia watched as Ruby left the lodge and wondered how she could get out of this. She shifted around on the dirt. "Does it get terribly hot in here?" she asked Cassandra. "I'm not a big fan of heat."

"You'll be fine," Cassandra said. "Don't focus on the heat. Focus on your breath. The heat will release all the toxins and impurities in your body. You'll feel fantastic after. I promise."

Sophia wasn't so sure about feeling fantastic. Already she was feeling faint. She watched as Ruby made several trips into the hovel with hot rocks. The lodge grew warm. Perspiration trickled down her legs and arms. Cassandra handed her a jug. "Have a sip of this. It'll help."

She sipped the pungent drink. Perspiration ran in rivers down her body. Ruby returned with one last rock, closed the tarp, and pulled out a small leather pouch. She sprinkled the fire with its contents. "This is cedar, Sophia. It will cleanse your negative thoughts." She pulled out two other pouches and sprinkled the glowing rocks. "These are tobacco and sage. They will bring you healing." The thick warm air grew heavy. Sophia closed her eyes. Trying not to focus on the excessive heat, she could feel her body begin to relax. Her mind slowed as Ruby and Cassandra chanted unfamiliar sounds.

Ruby spoke. "I want you to focus on your breath. Let the thoughts come and go. The Goddess of All is waiting. It is the Great Mother who gave birth to the cosmos and its inhabitants. She created the heavens and the earths and gave the power of creation to all women. Ancient women were better in touch with nature and didn't apologize for their aging bodies. When a woman became one who kept the blood, she was respected and revered in her tribe. Many years ago, the diva whom dwells in each woman was forced underground by men demanding their dominance. Today she lays buried deep in your soul. She wants to be reclaimed and revered, not nipped, tucked, and shot full of collagen and Botox." Ruby paused. "The Goddess of All thinks it's quite funny, but a waste of time and energy. Love your changing body, Sophia. The wrinkles, lines, age spots, and the soft muscle. You have earned them, for they are the result of a life well lived. Do not listen to pop culture. Greedy corporations exploit the weaknesses of aging women. Focus on what is important. Listen to the wisdom of those who have traveled before you, so you can relearn your true nature. Then you will instruct those who follow in your footsteps. This is the only way we can break the cycle." Ruby chanted words Sophia had never heard before. Cassandra joined in with her clear, strong voice. Sophia felt ill because of the intense heat and struggled with her breath.

"Open the door for Sophia. Show her what she needs to know," Ruby chanted.

Sophia bowed her head and prayed, something she had not done in many years. Time expanded, and she felt her spirit fill the sweat lodge.

Ruby threw open the heavy blankets and tarps and led Sophia by the hand out of the lodge. She pointed to the mountains. "See the signs of spring. It is the time of rebirth. You need to honor and embrace change. All life is change. Accept the change and listen carefully for the lessons. Honor the rhythms of the natural world and the rhythms of your divine body."

Sophia felt as if every drop of water had been squeezed from her body. She wobbled. Cassandra grabbed her. "We don't want you falling over. You did well. We were in the lodge for several hours."

She leaned against her aunt. "I feel cleansed. Thank you, Ruby."

"I'll be waiting for your return." Ruby kissed her gently on the cheek.

Chapter 8

Cassandra set a blue ceramic bowl filled with yogurt, sliced strawberries, and granola down on the kitchen table and handed Sophia a map with a trail highlighted in yellow. "I want you to try this hike today." She said as she winked at Dave.

Sophia picked up the map and studied it. "I hope I don't get lost."

Cassandra took her tea and sat across from her. "You won't have a problem. This trail circles the airport. You can't possibly get lost."

"I get lost easily." She grinned and told her aunt about the time she had gotten lost driving back from San Francisco. She had taken the wrong freeway exit and ended up in South Lake Tahoe, instead of Truckee. She dug her spoon into the mixture and took a bite. "This is good."

Dave glanced up from the paper. "Wasn't that woman attacked by a mountain lion on that trail last fall?"

Sophia gasped. "There are mountain lions around here?"

Cassandra glared at Dave. "Stop it. He's just teasing you, Sophia. And he thinks it's funny." She kicked him under the table.

Dave stroked the gray stubble on his chin. "Or perhaps she was hiking the Cathedral Rock trail? Or maybe it was Bell Rock. I seem to be having a senior moment."

"Dave Stewart. That's enough," Cassandra said sternly. "Don't traumatize her."

Dave winked at Sophia. "Got your heart rate up a bit, didn't I? I'm just kidding, kiddo. You're going to be fine. Just don't feed the animals."

"Dave. That's enough," Cassandra warned.

Sophia stared at her food. "If something happens to me, you'll find my will in the top drawer. I've left all my earthly belongings to the SPCA."

"That's a good choice," Dave said. "I've read they have a low overhead."

She ignored Dave's teasing and finished her breakfast, rinsed her bowl, and placed it in the dishwasher. She fingered the beaded bracelet she wore on her wrist. Her rational mind argued that the journey was a joke, something concocted by Cassandra to take her mind off her empty nest and pending divorce, but her heart urged her to follow the directions. She picked up her water bottle and car keys. "If I'm not back by dusk, send out the search party."

"We're taking the afternoon yoga class," Cassandra said. "You should be back in three hours." She followed her out to her car.

"You expect me to do yoga after this hike? We'll see." Sophia opened the car door. "I'm still confused on what a vortex is. How will I know when I've found one?"

Cassandra hugged her. "Just remember that a vortex is a place of increased energy. You can't point to a rock and say, 'That's a vortex.' It's not that simple. The energy is all around. You will feel it when you start hiking the trail." She kissed Sophia gently on the cheek. "When you first arrived, you were filled with doubt, indecision, and anger. Now you seem calmer. You're ready for this journey now."

"I had every right to be angry. Brad left me for another woman, who's young enough to be my daughter. I lost my job. My children don't need me anymore. I'm fifty and alone."

Cassandra reached for Sophia's hand. "You have to get over that anger. It's holding you back. Anger will create disease in your body. The real test of womanhood is when you stand alone on your foundation. It takes many years for a woman to become herself."

"If you say so, but it sucks." She kissed her aunt's cheek and climbed into the car. "If I'm not back by dark, you'll know I've been eaten by a wild animal."

Cassandra laughed. "You're too skinny. They only like the meaty ones."

"My luck I'll meet one who's on a diet." Sophia shot back with a grin and a heavy feeling of anxiety caused by what she had agreed to. It was a short drive to the Airport Mesa. She followed the map and parked in the tiny parking lot. She placed her sunglasses on and adjusted her hat. She didn't need anymore lines around her eyes. She reached for her water bottle.

There was only one other car in the parking lot. She locked the car door and proceeded to climb the steep trail. The temperature was warm. She inhaled the fresh air and plodded up the trail. The scenery was spectacular. Sandstone formations of red, beige, and orange rose majestically over the juniper bushes and pinion pines, all lying underneath a deep blue sky.

Her mind fell in rhythm with her footsteps. When she reached the top of the trail and gazed down, the town of Sedona could be seen. Cars traveling the roads looked like ants. She felt a heightened sense of perspective when she sat on a large granite boulder and drank from her water bottle. The tranquil mood was sharply interrupted by the feeling of perspiration sliding down her back. *Now what? Am I supposed to sit here and wait for something to happen? What's going to happen, anyways? Cassandra's been vague. And who is that beautiful woman in my dreams? Perhaps Cassandra's drugging me with that tea she's made me drink?*

Sophia twisted the beads on the bracelet and waited. Nothing happened. It was all a hoax, she mused as she closed her eyes and struggled to meditate. Never having been one for mystical experiences, she opened her eyes and yelled, "Okay, I'm here!"

But nothing happened.

She felt discouraged. She stood and stretched. *Wait until I see Cassandra. She's going to get a piece of my mind.*

However, just in case there was something to her aunt's strange ideas, Sophia continued walking the trail. With each footstep, she felt the energy of the earth. Was that a vortex? She focused on her footsteps. She had forgotten how much she enjoyed hiking. She had hiked with her first husband, but Brad had never enjoyed it. He said it was too dirty. How many other things had she given up for him?

Let's see. He didn't like camping—the dirt issue. She couldn't count the number of social engagements he refused to attend because he felt the people weren't of his social rank. Like lawyers had a social rank? Weren't they below used car salesmen? She remembered his anger when she told him the latest lawyer joke. Brad lacked a sense of humor.

He had forced her to sell her beloved home, the one she had raised her children in—the only one she had ever felt really at home in. Her protests fell on deaf ears and he moved them into one of those new areas with people full of their own self-importance. He didn't like to read, while she devoured books. Once she had tried to get him to read a book she thought he would enjoy so they would have something to discuss, but he just placed the book by his side of the bed and said he would read it when he had time. Eventually when the dust on the jacket grew thick, she moved the book into the den.

She loved making artistic objects and displaying her finished projects around the house, but he would move them into the garage when she wasn't home. He only wanted real art, whatever that was, in his house. She argued that it was her house, too, but he said he paid the bills so he could make the decisions.

She loved gardening and the feel of her hands working the warm earth. She couldn't recall ever seeing him get his manicured hands dirty. What kind of man got his nails manicured? He used to nag her about her nails. He said they embarrassed him. How could you paint and garden with fake nails?

Once she had been good at tennis, but he had always been too busy to play with her. She paused. Then why had she married him? Sex? No. Even that had been orderly and planned.

Sophia continued walking. In the distance, a jackrabbit sat in the middle of the path. She took several steps toward the rabbit, hoping it would move out of her way, but it didn't budge. He just sat in the middle of the path, his nose twitching. *Should I go around? Are jackrabbits harmful? Do they attack people, or even worse—eat them?*

The rabbit scratched his fur with his hind leg. "Do not be afraid, Sophia. I won't hurt you. I am a friend of the Goddess."

"Are you talking to me?" She stood stone-still and stared at the rabbit.

"It appears that way." His nose twitched.

Am I in some drug-induced flashback? There has to be something in the tea Cassandra and Ruby have been giving me. "But rabbits can't talk."

The rabbit looked startled. "I didn't know that."

She scratched her head. *Have I fallen into some fairy tale? Am I hallucinating?*

Suddenly a white cloud enveloped the animal and the dust on the path swirled. She covered her eyes, and then opened them. A beautiful woman of indeterminable age with flowing dark hair stood before her. She was dressed in a white buckskin shirt and pants and carried a satchel on her back. The woman smiled warmly and embraced her. "They call me White Buffalo Woman. Come and walk with me, Sophia. I have been waiting for you."

Sophia gazed into the woman's liquid black eyes and saw her own past mistakes and failures. She cringed as she witnessed her fights with Brad, her indifference to her mother, and the time she had left Katie waiting at ballet for an hour because she had lost track of the time at her easel. The woman smiled gently and offered her hand, leading Sophia down the path and to a clearing under several large rocks. "Do you understand that the entire universe is your relation? Do you see the interconnectedness of all this? I am worried for the future of women on this planet. I want to point you in the direction, so you may fulfill your destiny and become the messenger who spreads the word to all women."

Sophia attempted to speak, but words wouldn't form. *A messenger? What was that about?* She allowed the woman to lead her further down the path. They stopped beneath several tall, craggy rocks. The woman motioned her to sit on a ledge and pulled out a handmade pipe from her satchel, along with tiny white crystals. She drew a circle in the red dirt and laid the sparkling crystals in the shape of a cross. "This is sacred space—the earth and sky. This cross shows the four directions and points to the path you must walk to release your true nature."

The woman lit the pipe, raised it, uttered a prayer, then took a drag. The smoke encircled her head. The woman handed the pipe to Sophia. "You will walk upon the earth spreading the word. The earth is sacred for she is your mother and grandmother. The smoke from the pipe will carry your prayers to the Goddess. If she thinks they are in your best interest, she will grant them. The wooden stem of the pipe represents the male aspect and the red stone bowl represents the feminine, which is the womb of all creation. By smoking this pipe, you will be bound to all women who have walked before you, and you will carry the message to all women who follow behind." Sophia took the pipe from the woman, still confused about the message, but if this was a fairy tale she might as well play along. She took a puff, then coughed. "Take several more puffs," the woman urged.

Sophia continued to smoke, and the dizziness continued, but the woman's liquid black eyes urged her to continue. When she had had enough, she handed the pipe back.

The woman took a long drag and expertly blew the smoke out in circles. "I want you to listen carefully. You need to stop criticizing yourself when you make a mistake. You've made your share of mistakes, but that is part of being a woman." She smiled. "I remember making plenty of mistakes when I was in human form. That is the process. We have to make mistakes in order to arrive at truth. We must learn through experience to distinguish what is real and what is not. When a woman makes a mistake, she stops and analyzes it, talks to the Goddess, and asks for guidance. She doesn't beat herself up like you do. You've played the martyr role in this lifetime, and in order to proceed on this journey, you need to release that energy. It holds you back from your true potential. Examine the circle and crystals. You will stub your toes, bruise your ankles, and bump your knees along the journey. There will be times you will forget which way you are going. You will fall. Pick yourself up and keep going. You will be furious for being so stupid and awkward at times. Don't give up. Keep walking. Find your way back to your center." She pointed to the center of the circle. "Let me describe the journey you are about to begin."

Sophia stared at the woman. She was confused. A rabbit that turned into a woman, a message for women, a journey? *What have I been smoking?* But the woman sat serenely, radiating love. "Okay. I'm ready."

The woman grinned. "Good, because even if you weren't, I'd still push you down the path. You will meet other divas on the path. Some will present you with a kernel of wisdom; some will give you a task. Tuck the wisdom in your heart, complete the task, and master the concept. You need to stay resourceful and flexible. Stay connected to your inner self and the energy around you. Are you ready for your first task?" the woman asked.

Sophia nodded in a positive manner.

The woman smiled. "Good. Your first assignment is to release the martyr energy you've been carrying around in this lifetime. After you break this pattern, you will be given the next assignment. This is your initiation into the goddess realm where your soul dwells. Should you lose your way, or be in need of assistance, meditate on your bracelet and ask for help."

"But how do I do it?" Sophia felt confused. Couldn't this task have been something easy, like to say ten *Hail Marys* and ten *Our Fathers*? Was she really that much of a martyr?

The woman smiled. "You need to examine why you've used the martyr energy in the first place and let it go."

The woman leaned over and kissed Sophia gently on the forehead. Her form started to fade. "Wait!" Sophia urged. Don't go yet! Where do I go from here?"

"Just go down the road a piece," the woman whispered. "Turn left at the large red boulder with the tree growing out of its side. Follow the trail and it will take you to your car. I'll be watching you."

The apparition faded and she glanced down at the path. The jackrabbit sat where the woman had stood. The rabbit twitched its nose and scurried down the path. Sophia wiped her brow and glanced down at her bracelet. The lone white bead shimmered in the sunlight. She decided to follow the woman's directions, turning left at the boulder. She had a million questions to ask Cassandra.

"What did you put in that tea?" Sophia shrieked as she slammed the studio door behind her, then perched her hands on her hips and gave her aunt an icy stare.

Cassandra turned around, wiped her clay-stained hands on her jeans, and burst into laughter. "I see that the hike was a success."

Sophia sank into a chair, unlaced her tennis shoes, and slid them off her feet. "I met this jackrabbit that turned into a beautiful woman who called herself White Buffalo. Are you sure there's not something in that tea you keep giving me? All this feels like something right out of the sixties, and I'm Alice."

Cassandra grinned. "Why don't you explain what happened?"

"You'll have me committed."

"Then I'll have to commit myself and every other woman who's completed the journey."

As Sophia blurted out the story, she studied her aunt's face.

Cassandra smiled and nodded. "So your first assignment is to heal that martyr energy you've been dragging behind you in suitcases since you've been a little girl," Cassandra said. "So you really are the messenger. It is written in the stars, you know. It was decided long before you were born. Do you want some tea?"

"Is it going to make me see talking rabbits?"

"No. It's just something that will activate your memories. Cassandra went over to her hot plate and poured water into two mugs. She reached into the back of the cupboard and grabbed a tin of tea bags. She rummaged around, found what she was looking for, and dropped one in each mug. "Here," she said handing her a mug. "This should help you remember."

Sophia sipped the tea, which had a hint of peppermint. "This is good." She watched her aunt. *What am I a messenger of? How to survive life on your own at fifty? There are countless other women who can do that.*

"Drink the tea. Then I want you to remember where you picked up that energy you're still carrying around." Cassandra sat in the chair opposite Sophia, sipping her tea.

Sophia finished the tea and her mind calmed as the memories slowly waded in her consciousness. It seemed as if there had been no passage of time. She was wearing the dark, unbecoming uniform. The nun stood in front of the class, tapping her desk with the wooden ruler, admonishing the students for some minor infraction. Next she saw herself standing in line at the confessional patiently waiting her turn. In her child's mind, she lined up her sins, the same tired ones she had used for years. That particular day there was a new priest. She entered the dark confessional, knelt on the kneeler, and bowed her head. The priest opened the tiny window and asked for her sins. First she recited the mortal sins, they were the big ones, the ones that sent you on the express elevator to hell and stained your soul for eternity. Next came the venial sins. She had plenty of them. *I disobeyed my mother five times. I said the Lord's name in vain three times. I took a cookie from the cookie jar without asking.* She heard the priest's monotone voice absolve her and ask her to do better.

Next she was in high school, still wearing that god-awful uniform, and still sitting in church lining up her sins pondering eternal justice. Did God really sit on the golden throne with a long list of her infractions clipped to a board? If he really was omniscient like the nuns preached, hadn't he seen the time she had been in the back of Andrew's Chevy? Did he know that she liked it when Andrew went down on her? Did he know she would have gone all the way if that car hadn't pulled up behind them? Did he know that she had let many boys do the same thing? Did he know that she had had sex her first year in college with that sweet boy from Atlanta? Sex before marriage was one of the Church's biggest sins.

Sophia saw her wounded self and burst into tears. "I remember the nuns preaching, 'You'll only get into heaven by sacrificing. All good girls sacrifice. Good girls wait for marriage. It is holy to sacrifice yourself for others.'" She sniffled. "I believed what they said. I put everyone else's needs before mine."

"Did you get anywhere by being the martyr?" Cassandra asked gently.

Sophia let out a slow laugh. "No. My husband left me. My kids really don't seem to care, and I don't think I have any true friends. I tried to be the perfect wife and mother. Even my spices are organized alphabetically." She paused. "I think I did too much for my children and Brad. I became dependent on Brad. He took me for granted and walked all over me." She thought for a moment. "I've caused myself a great deal of unnecessary grief and guilt."

"Your scars run deep," Cassandra said. "Tomorrow we're going to the Chapel of the Holy Cross, so you can reconnect with your Catholic roots and heal that martyr energy."

"How is that going to help me?"

"You have to trust me on this. There is no other church like this." Cassandra stood. "This will help you uncover your divine diva. Most women are only divas in their dreams, but there's a part of all women who long to live the diva lifestyle. Diva's buy what they want, eat what they want, and wear what they want. Divas don't listen to others, only themselves. Release that martyr energy. It holds you back."

That afternoon Sophia's body was fluid in the yoga poses. She let her mind drift into a trance as she worked through the postures, and at the end of class she closed her eyes and relaxed. Trailing behind Cassandra out of the studio, she wiped her forehead and breathed in the heady smell of blooming flowers. "Doesn't the time change soon?"

"I think it's this weekend." Cassandra opened her arms wide and inhaled the fresh air. "Spring is my favorite time of the year, and I feel like celebrating. Let's go out to dinner. There's this charming little Italian place that serves a marvelous polenta with a sauce of wild mushrooms. And tomorrow, after you've visited the chapel, we'll take that pink jeep tour. I'll make a reservation when we get home."

"Do I really have to go to this chapel?" she asked. She was afraid the roof would collapse when she walked into a church. It had been that long.

"You have to trust me on this," Cassandra said. "I, too, had to go there early in my journey."

"I didn't realize the Church got to you, too."

"Your mother and I were sent to Catholic boarding school, because our mother didn't want to deal with us during the school year. It interfered with her busy social calendar. She also wanted to make sure that we were good little Catholic girls." Cassandra giggled. "Little did she know that the school was a haven for drinking and sex." Her face grew pale. "That was a long time ago. I'd rather not discuss it."

Chapter 9

Cassandra drove up to a white gate, stopped, and rolled down the window. An elderly man dressed in a pale blue turtleneck and tan slacks poked his head into the car. "Hi, Tom," she said. My niece is visiting from Reno, and I want to show her the chapel."

Tom poked his head into the car and smiled warmly. "Welcome, Miss. Is this your first time to the chapel?"

Sophia nodded, still feeling apprehensive.

"May you find what you're looking for, and may the energy heal your soul. Cassandra, will we see you next week at the council meeting?"

"You're involved in city government?" Sophia asked.

"Don't be so shocked. Sometimes a woman has to do what she has to do." Cassandra nodded at Tom. "I'll be there. Dave said he'd come, too. He's worried about the impact that new road will have."

"Great. We'll see you there. Enjoy your visit." Tom waved them through the gate. Cassandra drove up the steep hill and parked. The parking lot was filled with cars and several tour buses.

"Why are all these people here?" Sophia asked.

"There's something special about the chapel. You'll see for yourself. The chapel doesn't just attract Catholics, but people from every faith. When I first moved to Sedona, I visited weekly because the energy is so healing. Come, follow me." Cassandra led the way up a sharp walkway, into a plaza and pointed to two rock pillars. "These are called *The Nuns.*"

Sophia studied the pillars. "Hmm." She squinted, visualizing Sister Marie and Sister Celeste from her high school days. They had stood sentry outside the girls' bathroom, waiting to catch them smoking.

Cassandra pointed to another thin pillar. "See that one. When the woman who built the chapel first saw that rock, she decided it looked like Mary holding the baby Jesus. She named it *Madonna and Child*. It was then that she decided to build the church on the hillside and dedicate it to the memory of her parents."

Sophia looked around the plaza and saw the entrance to the church. It fit into the red rock landscape discretely, as if it had been designed by a higher power. "Come, follow me." Cassandra guided her to the entrance. "This is where the magic occurs. This is like no church you've ever seen."

They entered through the heavy wooden doors and walked into a large foyer. Sophia gasped as she stared at the large glass windows that looked out over the red rocks. Cassandra was right. This was quite a unique church. There were no crucifixes or statues of saints. Simple tapestries hung from the walls. "It's breathtaking." She stood in awe, realizing she was in the presence of the Divine. Without planning to, she bowed humbly.

"I come here often," Cassandra said. "Come, follow me and we'll find a seat."

The familiar sounds and smells from her childhood religion were strangely comforting. She followed her aunt, dipping her fingers into the holy water and anointing her body, making the sign of the cross, and mumbling the customary words. She genuflected and slipped into one of the wooden pews, staring out the tall windows and into the beauty of the red rocks. A wooden untrimmed altar faced the pews. Hanging over the altar was a simple piece of art. It was as if the architect had envisioned the creation of the church in a dream and sculpted it to fit discretely into the landscape.

Sophia sat next to her aunt. The church was crowded. Tourists snapped pictures. The faithful prayed, and others stood and stared at the beautiful simplicity. She leaned against the back of the wooden pew, closed her eyes and let the feeling of peace and contentment engulf her very soul. Using the breathing she had learned in yoga, she inhaled deeply and mentally recited the familiar prayers of childhood. She remembered the time when priests had spoken in mysterious Latin and swung their incense lanterns around the church. She slipped into a trance.

"Blessed are you among women," a gentle voice whispered.

Sophia opened her eyes, blinked, and glanced around the chapel. It was strangely empty. She heard the sound of heavenly music. Hovering above the altar was the apparition of a woman cloaked with the radiance of the sun. The woman smiled benevolently, rays of pink and white shooting off in various directions. "Do not be afraid, Sophia," the woman said. "I have a gift for you. Please close your eyes."

Sophia shivered as she gazed into the woman's pale blue eyes. She felt uncertain, but the woman smiled gently. She closed her eyes. A movie reel played in Technicolor. She saw herself as a little girl, listening to the words of the church elders, standing in line at the confessional, lining up her sins like she lined up the dolls in her room. Next she was with a visiting priest in the tiny hall closet in the basement of the school. The image of the priest came in jagged pieces. She grimaced as she watched his large hands travel up her uniform and finding her panties. She opened her eyes and cried, "I tried to stop him." She didn't want to watch this any longer. "But I couldn't. He was much bigger and stronger. He said it was my job to please him, and I would be rewarded in heaven for my obedience. He threatened me that if I told another person he'd tell God and I would go straight to hell."

The woman sat next to her, picked up her hand, and held it gently in her own. "It's okay to cry. I've shed many tears for you and all the other children exploited by church elders.

It was wrong what that priest did, but you can't judge the entire church by the actions of a few. Most of the men and women who serve the church are humble, good souls."

Tears streamed down Sophia's face. Father Joe—she had never forgotten him. "I tried to tell my mother that afternoon, but she ignored what I said and made me take a bath. The following day she said it never happened. To this day I remember her words, 'A priest would never do that.' We never talked about it again."

"What the priest did was wrong. It wasn't your fault," the woman said. You did nothing to provoke him. It pains me that you are still holding on to that energy. You need to release it and forgive the priest. It is not healthy for you to carry around that baggage."

Sophia stared at the woman. "I was only a little girl. I still don't understand why he would do that to a child."

"It is not our business to try and understand. He will pay for his actions. You are responsible for forgiving him." She smiled serenely. "That is all you have to do."

"How do I forgive him?"

"Ask and you will receive."

Sophia stared at the beautiful woman and bowed her head in prayer. "I forgive you, Father Joe," she whispered. "I forgive you." After saying the words, she felt strangely lighter, freer than she had in years. She closed her eyes and recited prayers for the others who had been victimized by the church. She finished and leaned back into the pew and opened her eyes.

The apparition of the heavenly woman floated in front of her. "You have shown compassion," the woman said. "That is good. Do not hold resentments or judgments for they poison your soul. Learn to forgive those who trespass against you, or you will stagnate on your journey. Religions often mirror a culture's devaluation of women. Sophia, I want you to remember this: A woman who has activated her diva power

105

cares for all, regardless of religion, political viewpoint, nationality, race, gender, creed, or skin color."

Sophia nodded. "I understand."

"That is good. Practice loving kindness and you will develop inner peace. Attachments and aversions cause suffering. Those who have harmed you will have to atone for their actions before they can proceed on their own journeys. A diva shows compassion to those who have harmed her and to those who ache. Remember this in times of despair. You are wearing the bracelet. That is good." The woman leaned over and kissed her tenderly on the cheek.

Sophia watched as the woman faded into the light, feeling a shift in her soul.

"Wake up." Sophia felt a tug at her arm and opened her eyes. She was lying on the stone floor. Cassandra stood over her with a worried look on her face. "You fell over. You had me worried. Are you okay?"

Two older gentlemen leaned over the pew. "You had us scared, Miss," the man with the gray mustache said. "Do you need a doctor?"

She shook her head and checked her body for aches. "I'm fine. I think I just had a divine experience."

The two men exchanged glances. "You have a nasty bump on your head," one of the men said. "You might want to get that checked out."

"I'll be fine. Thank you." Sophia leaned against her aunt. "I'd like to go home now."

Cassandra led her out of the church, down the walkway, and to the car. She opened the door and helped her in.

"I need to come back here. Something magical happened," Sophia mumbled.

"You can come anytime you want. The church is open from nine to five."

Sophia pulled the mirror down and rubbed her bump. She was going to have a nasty bruise. "Do they celebrate Mass here?"

"No, they stopped saying Mass years ago because it got too crowded." She smiled, then backed out the car being careful to avoid the throngs of people. "I think we'll take a pink jeep tour another day." Sophia dozed on the ride back. She allowed Cassandra to lead her into the bedroom, remove her shoes, and help her into bed. "I'll be in my studio if you need me," Cassandra said, as she quietly closed the door.

Sophia fell into a deep sleep, her dreams vibrant. In one dream she was a snake, slithering in the hot sun on a cluster of red rocks. She felt her skin molt and slip off, giving birth to a smooth shiny new skin.

"Well, hello, sleepyhead," Cassandra said. She stood at the foot of the bed with a tray.

Sophia opened her eyes and stretched. She felt deliciously rejuvenated. "What time is it? I feel like I've slept for days."

Cassandra set the tray down and sat at the edge of the bed. "You've been asleep for about twenty hours. I've checked on you periodically, but let you sleep. Obviously you needed it. Here, let me help you." She plumped up the pillows and helped Sophia up, then handed her a mug of tea.

After her initial grogginess had passed, she suddenly remembered the encounter with the heavenly woman. "I can't remember the last time I slept that long."

"How do you feel?"

She took an inventory of her body by wiggling her toes and giving her neck a good stretch. She felt for the bump on her head, but it was gone. "Fine. I think I'd like to visit your serenity room."

Cassandra smiled, led her down the hallway, and opened the door to the room. "I'll be in the kitchen if you need me."

Sophia headed directly to the altar. She lit several candles, sat cross-legged on a floor cushion, and watched the flames flicker. She closed her eyes, recited a daisy chain of familiar prayers, and concentrated on her breathing as she released the martyr energy and ghosts from the past that she had dragged around for decades.

That afternoon Sophia accompanied Cassandra on one of the pink jeep tours of the Red Rocks. Their tour guide, an affable man named Peter who had come to Sedona after college twenty years before and never left, took them on a wild ride over the rough terrain. Sophia leaned against the railing and listened as their trip mates, a couple from the Midwest, chatted with Cassandra. Several times they attempted to include her. She answered quickly, then reverted to silence, drinking in the beauty of the surroundings as the jeep bounced along the rutted roads. She watched as the hue of the roads gradually shifted from an orange-tinged ocher to a deep red. She tried to listen as Peter explained the terrain, but her mind wandered. She stood for pictures when asked, and by the time the tour was finished and her bottom was sore from the jarring ride, her experience at the chapel had crystallized in her soul.

Peter pulled up to the office, they scrambled out of the jeep, thanked their guide and said goodbye to their travel companions. As they walked up the hill, Sophia said, "I feel much clearer."

They stopped on the street. The sun had set and the rocks were inky black. Crowds of people were out shopping and socializing. Cassandra tilted her head, studied the look on Sophia's face, and then grinned. "The energy around you has shifted. Tomorrow you will visit Bell Rock."

Chapter 10

"I think it would be wise for you to take this particular hike at twilight," Cassandra said.

"I'm scared of hiking alone in the dark," Sophia admitted.

"You will be protected. I promise. Take this flashlight. The trail is circular. You will arrive back where you started."

Reluctantly, Sophia followed her aunt's instructions. She drove to the parking lot, laced up her shoes, and gathered the flashlight and cell phone, then wrapped courage around her body like a shawl. "I'm not afraid. I'm not afraid," she recited as she walked. She had always had a hard time with the dark. At night, even when Brad was home, she had lit the house up like a mall at Christmas. It was always in the dark when her demons surfaced.

As she hiked the trail, she observed the darkening terrain. Time stood still in the Red Rocks. The tall majestic rocks Mother Nature had carved out in a fury of energy seemed to stretch to the heavens. She inhaled the clean, fresh, and invigorating air. No gardeners needed here. Mother Nature did all the pruning herself. Trails crisscrossed the well-trodden path as she walked. Scattered pine needles carpeted the earth and the sky darkened.

She reflected back to the woman in the chapel and remembered the incident with Father Joe. Over the long ensuing years, she had tried to forget the incident, but it was always there—lurking in the back of her mind. The embarrassment and horror she had experienced never left. She remembered soaking in a hot bath that night, trying to scrub away the smell of his body and the stain of his fingers. She convinced her mother she had the flu and stayed home from school for several days. When she returned to school, she discovered that he had left. *How many other girls or boys had he molested? No child should have to suffer the indignity that she had endured,* she thought as she continued hiking.

She had kept her secret hidden in her heart. She had a hard time admitting her problems. There was a part of her that pretended life was perfect and the incident had never occurred. She was still angry at her mother. She should have protected her. She should have listened and stormed down to the school and demanded an investigation. She would have done that for Katie or Ben.

But Sophia believed her mother had never liked her, and she had built her world around that.

As her feet crunched on the path, she remembered all the silly little rules her mother had drilled into her head. "Separate your clothes into categories. Red hangers for short-sleeve tops, blue for long-sleeve tops. Always wear clean underwear in case you're in an accident. Ladies never chew gum." And those stupid seven-days-a-week panties she had worn under her school uniform as a young girl! God forbid she ever wore Monday's panties on Tuesday.

Her mother's advice hadn't stopped in childhood. Along with wardrobe suggestions, she sent her advice on how to clean her house, shop for groceries, and discipline her children. Once she told her she was too bland and needed to add color to her life. After Sophia received that advice, she painted her bathroom red and sent her mother a picture of it.

There were her daughter's criticisms. "You shouldn't wear those pants, Mom. You look ridiculous. You can't get a belly button ring. You're too old for a tattoo. Your skin will sag. Why can't you be like other mothers and dress your age?" But she had never been one for pressed shirts and pants. She favored jeans, funky tops with flowing sleeves, dangling earrings, and Birkenstocks.

Sophia continued hiking and thought about her son. Ben had never criticized her wardrobe or her hair. When he was only four, he said she was the most beautiful woman in the world. He wanted to marry her when he grew up. She explained that she was married to his father and she couldn't marry him. He had burst into tears and said he was never going to leave her.

As the wind picked up, a powerful thought floated through her mind. What if mature women staged a revolution? What if they took back the culture? What had happened to her generation? They were going to take the world by storm and reinvent the rules. They had been activists, protesting the war and injustices of the government. They had burned their bras and marched for equal pay for equal work. Look at them now! They all drove BMW's, lived in the suburbs, stood in line at Starbucks, and worried about their stock portfolios.

She stopped, uncapped her water bottle, and took a drink. It was strange that there was no one else on the trail. She shone her flashlight down the trail and saw a large boulder. She went over and sat, took out a scarf, and wiped her face. She watched as the birds darted through the trees.

"Sophia, I have been waiting for you."

She turned around, shivers crept up her spine. There was no one there.

"Sophia."

She glanced up. A raven sat on a tree branch. She quivered as she remembered Poe's famous poem. "Are you talking to me?"

The raven swooped down and stood on the path. Suddenly, it transformed into a three-faced elderly woman. She gasped. "Do not be afraid," the old woman said. "I am Hecate. I see in all directions: the past, the present, and the future. I represent wisdom, knowledge, and joy that all middle-aged women desire. I symbolize the time when the moon withholds its light before emerging into the night sky."

Sophia glanced around. There was no moon, yet it was light. She stared at the woman.

"This light represents the light that you hold inside yourself. This inner light can illuminate your life as well as the lives of others," the woman said. "I see the path that brought you here and the roads you might take." The woman waved her hand and three paths emerged, all leading in different directions. "There are many trails to choose from, but you must choose carefully. You are a spiritual woman on a spiritual path. You need to answer this question before you can proceed further: What did I come here to do?"

Sophia thought for a moment. "I raised two children. I was a good attentive wife. I took care of the house and garden. I cooked all the meals, made sure everyone had clean clothes. I drove the carpool, took the kids to their appointments, and attended every game and PTA meeting. I even had a job. What else was I supposed to do?"

The three-headed woman nodded. "Yes, you did all that. You did a wonderful job, I might add. But your children are grown, your marriage is over, and you've lost your job. Your husband is a jerk. He's not worthy of you. You never liked your job. You weren't honoring your soul with that kind of work. You are destined to do something else."

The truth stung. Sophia wiped her eyes. "You're brutally honest."

The three-headed woman nodded. "There is no purpose in withholding the truth. You need to speak your truth and rebirth yourself into the creative phase of your life. You are no longer responsible for your children, your husband, or your past. You have released your martyr energy. It is time for your next assignment."

"Isn't this going too quickly? I've just released the martyr energy. Don't I need some time to adjust?"

The woman shook her head. "You will stop the momentum. Your assignment this time is to stop withholding the truth about your marriage. You've never spoken up about your husband's abuse. You've danced around the topic in your counseling sessions."

Sophia didn't know what to say. She was stunned. *How does this woman know about that? But then here I am stuck in some fairy tale and talking to a woman with three heads.* "I was too ashamed. I thought I deserved it."

The three-headed woman shook her head. "No woman deserves abuse. Watch this with me." She waved her hand and a movie screen suddenly appeared. Sophia watched herself and Brad through the years. She cringed as she witnessed all the times he had squeezed her arm too tightly and left bruises. She winced as she witnessed the times he slapped her across the face, and the time he punched her in the stomach. She saw her kids hide behind the couch as he threw his verbal attacks.

The film stopped. "I didn't know the kids saw any of this. I didn't want anyone to know. I was too embarrassed." The tears flooded her eyes.

"You have had this problem since you were abused by the priest," the three-headed woman said. "You never thought you were a woman with value. You let your husband walk all over you. You let your mother dominate you. The first time you ever stood up for yourself was when you saw your husband and that woman in the restaurant." She smiled. "I was right behind you."

Sophia gasped. "I've wondered what came over me. It wasn't like me to make a scene in a public place." She smiled. "Thank you. I felt like I was in control."

The three-headed woman nodded. "See the three paths before you. Examine them. Which path has heart? Do you have the courage to take it?"

Sophia studied the three paths. "I think I'll take the middle path."

"That is good. That is the path you are supposed to take. Listen carefully. You need to speak the truth. It is time for you to let go of your marriage. It does not honor your soul. You are entering the third phase of your life, which is the creative phase. The creative phase is attached to the deepest part of your soul. You have a great deal of work to do because you are now fifty."

Sophia sighed. "Yes. I'm old." She looked at the woman, who had to be a hundred. "I'm sorry."

"Do not say you're sorry. I am old. I have been around for hundreds of years. You are speaking the truth. This is important. Please listen carefully. You are being reborn into the creative phase of life, but with rebirth bring death to your former way of life. You give up the ability to have children. The finality of your youth is over. You now hold the life-giving powers within you, like the moon. In the past, women at this stage of life were valued and honored in their communities. They held powers and skills that younger women could not possess. Cassandra plans to give you a croning ceremony when you become a juicy crone."

Sophia felt puzzled. "What's a crone?"

"A crone is a woman who has journeyed through menopause, which is the third stage of being a woman. It is the initial step to becoming a diva." The woman raised her arms to the sky. "A diva has zest, passion, and soul. She is in Act III of her life. She is the wise woman. She nurtures growth. You are good at gardening, Sophia. Now it is time to prune, weed, and plant your own soul. It is time for you to give back, but first you must speak your truth. Once you speak your truth, you need to plan your future."

Sophia hated to admit it, but the three-headed woman made sense. "I need to speak my truth to Brad and get what's fair in the divorce."

The three-headed woman smiled. "Yes. That is your assignment. Speak up for yourself. Demand what is yours and be fair." She leaned over and kissed her. It is time for you to go back."

"How do I get out of here?"

"Just go down the middle trail a piece. Turn left at the large boulder and follow the path to your car. I will illuminate the way."

The three-headed woman vanished. The raven sat in the trail. He cawed once and flew away.

She followed the middle trail. It led her to her car.

There was a knock on Sophia's bedroom door. "That husband of yours is on the phone. He says it's important," Cassandra said. "Do you want me to tell him you're not here?"

Sophia wrapped her robe tightly around her body and opened the door. "I guess it's time," she said.

Her aunt handed her the phone. "Do what you need to do."

Sophia took the phone and stared at it. She gathered her courage and spoke, "What do you want?"

"I'm sending some papers down for you to sign."

"And exactly what papers am I supposed to sign?"

Brad cleared his throat, obviously from nervousness. "I'm putting the house on the market, and I'm starting divorce proceedings. If you cooperate, I'll make it easy on you."

"Well, that's big of you. Always thinking of me."

"Let's not go there, Sophia."

She chuckled. "I gather Leslie doesn't want to live in our house."

"How did you know?"

"Oh, just a woman's intuition. I don't blame her. The house has no soul. Do what you like. I never liked that house anyways."

"I never meant to hurt you, Sophia," Brad said softly.

"I'm sure, Brad. It just happened. Just like all the times you hit me, or called me names. You didn't mean to." There she said it. Over the air waves. It was out in the open.

"I don't know what you're talking about."

"Let's not play the denial game anymore, because if you do, I'll file spousal abuse charges. I'm not going to be silent anymore."

He stuttered. "You...you have no proof. It would be your word against mine. What judge is going to believe you anyway? You're just the crazy woman who ran away."

"The kids saw, Brad. They'll back me up."

"The kids never saw anything. You're making this up."

"They did see. I want you to listen carefully because I'm only going to say this once, Counselor. Do not call me again. I will hire a lawyer and we will only confer through our lawyers. I am divorcing you. If you push me, I'll tell everyone about your temper. I'm sure Leslie would like to know that little, dark side of you. All I want is my car, my clothes, the photo albums, and fifty thousand dollars. You finish paying the kids' college tuition and take care of their health care."

"I don't have fifty thousand to give you."

"You will when the house sells."

"But that will be most of the equity. Don't you remember we took out that second mortgage for college tuitions?" he asked, his voice sounding weak.

"It wasn't only for college. If I remember you used some of the money for your golf membership. So that's the deal. You get Leslie and that ugly furniture you had to have and I get the money. Otherwise, I'll blow your cover. How will it look to have a prominent attorney sued for spousal abuse?"

"This isn't like you," Brad said. "What's come over you? It's your aunt. She's corrupted your thinking."

"No. I'm thinking quite clearly now. I'll expect those papers tomorrow. I recommend Candice Booth to sell the house. She's an aggressive agent. She'll sell the house quickly. If it doesn't sell quickly, I'll have to tell Leslie about your deep secrets."

"You're a bitch."

"Keep it up, Brad. It'll cost you more money. I wonder what you're esteemed colleagues and neighbors will think when they find out that you like to use your fist when you don't get your way. That'll be great gossip on the golf course."

"You're bluffing."

"Then try me. My lawyer will contact you." She hung up, feeling empowered for the first time in her marriage.

That night an old woman appeared in her dreams. Her black eyes glittered, her face wrinkled and caved-in where teeth should have been. Bony and bent over with age, she was dressed in dark, ratty clothes and carried a long stick. She shook the stick at Sophia. The woman reminded her of one of the wicked old witches from the fairy tales of her childhood. The woman came closer and scrunched her face. "You have spoken your truth. That is why I am here. I was sent by Hecate. I will not harm you. I am not the wicked old witch, but the harvest goddess, Baba Yaga. I not only harvest grain but women. I plant women, raise them, cut them down, and store them all through the dark winter's night. In the spring, I replant them again. You are being replanted, Sophia. I have done all I can do to help you. You need to take charge of your physical health. You have starved yourself for too long. It is time to stop punishing yourself. Look to your bracelet for guidance."

Chapter 11

Sophia took Cassandra's advice and went to see Joan Brandt, a lawyer who specialized in divorces. Joan sat across the desk from her and asked a series of questions. What had she brought into the marriage? Had he ever strayed before? Did they have joint accounts? How active was he in the child rearing? How much money had she earned? Sophia answered as Joan jotted the answers down on a legal pad. "I have a friend I went to law school with who lives in Las Vegas," Joan said. "She'll do the filing. I'll act as your conduit down here." She studied Sophia. "After twenty-three years of marriage you're entitled to a lot more than fifty thousand dollars and your car. Are you sure you don't want to go after more? Let's throw in attorney fees."

That was a good idea. She knew how expensive attorneys were. Over the years, she had watched Brad submit his billable hours. "Okay. Go for that, but I don't want anything else. I just want a clean break from the jerk. As long as he pays for the children's education, I'll be fine." She watched as Joan wrote and judged her to be around her own age. She was dressed very business-like in a navy blue suit with her brown hair pulled back in a clip.

"In your state, you're entitled to reconstructive alimony," Joan said. "Are you sure you don't want to go for that? It would give you several years of income to retrain in another field."

"You might want to put that as a side note if he doesn't agree. Brad can be quite nasty." Sophia twisted her hands. "I just want to go forward and have nothing to do with him again."

Joan smiled. "Unfortunately, it will not be that simple. There will be your children's graduations, weddings, and grandchildren. When there are children involved, we're never quite finished with our ex-spouses."

"I realize that. I've seen enough friends go through divorces."

Joan stood. "Okay. I have all the information I need. I will send the petition up tomorrow, and we'll get started."

"Thank you for helping me."

"It's my pleasure. I've been where you are. I remember the pain." Joan walked her to the door. "Have a good day."

Sophia hurried to her car. She had another appointment. When she had told Cassandra about the woman in her dreams, she had made an appointment with a doctor. "But she isn't your average doctor," Cassandra said. "You'll love her."

She followed the directions and found herself pulling in front of a small building. Tiny silver bells jingled as she entered the office. A young girl, who must have been around Ben's age, with short blond hair and multiple earrings in her ears, glanced up from her desk. "May I help you?"

"I'm Sophia Roberts. I have a two o'clock appointment with Doctor Myers."

The girl checked the appointment book. "She'll be with you in a moment." She handed Sophia a clipboard with several papers attached and a pen. Please fill these out."

She took the clipboard and pen from the young girl and glanced around the small office. Macramé wall hangings were artfully arranged on cream-colored walls. Sounds of gentle music filled the air. A table was filled with tiny tubes of oil. She walked over and picked one up and took a whiff of sweet lavender. A collection of tapes and books for sale filled a large bookcase. She perused the book selections. There were multiple volumes on Chinese medicine, women's issues, health, and menopause. She picked up a thick purple book that looked interesting. If she had enough time after she finished the paperwork, she just might skim it.

"Sophia, I'm Adrienne Myers." A tall elegant woman with straight brown hair flecked with gray stood before her. A long white coat covered a denim dress. She wore sensible brown shoes. The woman smiled and extended her hand.

Sophia capped the pen. "It's nice to meet you." She shook the woman's warm hand. "My aunt recommended you."

"What's your aunt's name?"

"Cassandra Morris."

Doctor Myers grinned. "A vibrant woman. She comes in several times a year. She takes wonderful care of herself."

"She's been taking great care of me. I arrived at her doorstep a mess."

Sophia followed Doctor Myers in the office and she motioned for her to take a seat as she took the papers from her. "What can I do for you today?"

Sophia rung her hands, wondering if she should tell her about this journey she was on. She spied the woman's medical degrees hanging on the wall and decided against it. "It's been recommended that I improve my physical health. In the past, I've struggled with anorexia. While I'm not really anorexic any more, I need to learn to eat better. I still resist letting myself eat and enjoy food. I haven't had a period in over a year, and I don't take any hormones."

Doctor Myers jotted down some notes. "How do you feel about taking hormones?"

"I'm not sure. I've read conflicting literature, but I have a gut feeling synthetic estrogen is not for me. My doctor back home didn't listen and tried to force me to take hormones. He said if I don't take them I'll shrivel up and be hunched over." She paused for a moment while Doctor Myers wrote. "I threw the prescription away. I'd like my vitality back. My issues with anorexia have haunted me for years. I'm concerned I'm losing bone mass."

"You are awfully thin. Do you know how much you weigh?"

"About one hundred and two pounds." She didn't want to admit that the last time she weighed herself she was wearing shoes, jeans, a turtleneck, and a jacket.

Doctor Myers looked concerned. "That's not enough for your frame. I recommend you gain at least ten pounds. I'm certain you'll find increased energy, and you'll feel younger."

Sophia gasped. "Ten pounds! I'll look fat." Cassandra had already made her gain five pounds. The old demons from her past surfaced, taunting her.

Doctor Myers smiled gently. "No, Sophia. You'll look wonderful. The dangers of anorexia are severe. You're starving your body. When the body doesn't have enough nutrients, it attacks the inner organs." She glanced down at her sheets. "You wrote here that you are separated. For how long?"

Sophia paused. When did she start counting? From the moment she saw Brad and Leslie in the restaurant, or when she left home? She shrugged. "It's been about six weeks. My husband cheated on me with a younger woman. He wants to marry her and have a baby." She laughed. "He was never very good with our children."

"I'm sure that hurts," Doctor Myers said. "It sounds like he's experiencing a mid-life crisis."

"I think he's been having one for the last five years." Sophia explained the sports car, new wardrobe, and fancy house.

Doctor Myers nodded, writing down notes. "Separation causes stress in the body. I read your questionnaire and according to Oriental medicine, I would classify you as an Earth type. I imagine throughout your life you have been the peacemaker in situations. You spent a great deal of energy worrying about things that you had no control over. I gather you are more comfortable giving attention to others than receiving. Your lifelong struggle to control your weight suggests a fondness with the Earth."

Sophia blushed. The doctor had her pegged. For years she had worried about everything—nuclear holocaust, the depletion of the ozone layer, meteors hitting the earth, giant earthquakes that would swallow her, and terrorism. "Yes, but…" *Would this woman understand?*

Doctor Myers grinned. "You are in the red rocks to release your diva power. It's written all over your aura. I bet you've met Hecate."

Sophia nodded, indicating that she had.

"Good. I deal with many women like you. They find themselves at the crossroads. Their nests are empty. Many of their marriages are over, either due to divorce or death, and they are lost. They don't know which fork in the road to travel."

"What do I do now?" Sophia asked.

"You must take care of your health so you may enter the third phase of life. I agree with you about synthetic hormones. The drugs promised youth and femininity forever, without exploring its dark side. Now we know the truth. Uterine cancer, breast cancer, liver disease, endometriosis…" Doctor Myers sighed. "The list goes on. I disagree with modern medicine's way of medicating women as we gain our true power. There was a saying when I was in medical school. 'Better living through chemistry.'" She laughed. "We were taught that menopause was an estrogen-deficiency disease, and it could be controlled with expensive drugs. You don't need any of that. I can suggest herbs that will help you and several topical creams."

Sophia glanced at the walls where several diplomas hung in their gold frames. She squinted and recognized the name of a top medical school.

Doctor Myers capped her pen and closed the folder. "I chose to study Oriental Medicine, because I didn't like the way doctors treated female problems in medical school. I'm about ten years older than you. I went through the change about eight years ago and I'm living without synthetic hormones. My mother, who's in her eighties, has never taken hormones. She still works. She's a doctor, also. She plays golf, tennis, practices yoga and hasn't lost an inch in height. I agree with Margaret Mead that the zest of a post-menopausal woman is phenomenal. It shouldn't be controlled with medication, but rather released into society to benefit mankind.

"I teach women to help themselves. Your symptoms will not disappear overnight because I don't dispense pills that mask the problems. When a woman's need is to solve other people's problems, it leaves her emptied. In your case, this, coupled with the fact that you haven't eaten properly for decades, has thrown your body completely off balance. I suggest you get your body in balance, so you can release your diva power and find some meaningful work. I noticed you've turned fifty. I imagine when you're ready, your aunt will give you a croning ceremony, which is a woman's initiation into her wisdom years." She smiled. "I've been to several of your aunt's ceremonies. She does a spectacular job initiating women into the ancient sisterhood of the wise women."

"I've never thought of myself as a wise woman."

Doctor Myers smiled gently. "You have all the necessary ingredients. Now, I'd like to perform acupuncture on you to release you inner demons."

"My inner demons?" *Could she see them dancing around her head?* "Acupuncture?" *I hate needles!*

"Acupuncture will release the negative energy you've stored in your body for decades and open up your meridians so your chi can flow smoothly. You'll love it."

"What's chi and what's a meridian?"

"In Chinese medicine, chi means life. It is the vital spark that infuses matter with energy. Chi gives you energy to live your life," Doctor Myers explained. "Thousands of years ago the Chinese devised a map of the human body and identified sixteen major meridians of invisible channels in which chi flows. By strategically placing needles in these meridians, I can restore your chi. Oftentimes chi is blocked due to emotional issues. Come, follow me. I promise you it won't hurt."

Sophia gathered her purse and followed the doctor down a narrow hall and into a darkened room. Water trickled from a tabletop fountain. The room was tastefully decorated with pictures and statues. An examining table dominated the center of the room. "I need your shoes, socks, watch, and bracelet off. Please lay face up." Sophia followed the instructions and scooted up on the table. Doctor Myers placed a cassette in the machine and relaxing music played. "I need to wash my hands," she said. "I'll be right back."

Sophia lay on the table and stared at the ceiling, focusing on a small stain by the light. Her hands felt sweaty. She remembered taking Ben and Katie to the doctor for their shots. She had feigned stoicism as the nurse held the large silver needle, so she held their tiny hands and looked the other way.

Doctor Myers returned. "Good. You're ready." She unwrapped the tiny needles. "Now you're going to feel a tiny poke. These needles are much smaller than the regular ones." She moved up and down Sophia's body, placing the needles at various points. Several times Sophia flinched, but then the minuscule pain subsided. "I'm going to set the timer for thirty minutes," Doctor Myers said. "I want you to close your eyes and take long, slow breaths through your nose and exhale through your mouth. Free the mind from all thought. I'll be back when the time is up."

At first, Sophia didn't feel a thing. Was this another gimmick that proved to be a bust? She thought about other gimmicks she had tried over the years. Creams that promised to erase the lines of time, lotions to smooth the skin, highlights added to the hair. Several years before she had tried one of the popular injectables promised by the dermatologist to combat crow's feet. For several months she looked surprised, but then the stubborn lines returned.

A few minutes later she felt a wave of energy. She closed her eyes and relaxed with the soothing music. She journeyed into the star-filled heavens, the beams of colored light connected to various parts of the galaxy. As she flew, the sun exploded into a rainbow of whirling light. She found herself in the grand court of a palace with exquisitely polished marble floors and flowing fountains. The sweet-smell of flowers filled the air. A swirling ball of light approached her and took form. The beautiful woman dressed in a white flowing gown smiled and held out her hand. "I am always with you. Come, I have something to show you."

Sophia took the woman's outstretched hand. They glided through the castle and into a large room. In the center stood a tall pedestal. A thick leather book sat on top. "I have something to show you," the beautiful woman said. She pointed to the gilded book with gold embossed lettering. "This is the *Book of Women*. On these pages are the good deeds done by women since the beginning of time. The beautiful woman flipped through the pages and pointed to a name: Sophia Snider Roberts. Daughter, mother, wife. The following words blurred. Sophia's eyes couldn't focus on the text. "It is against the law of the Goddess not to heal your wounds, follow your heart's desire, and release your power. This is what you were born to do." The woman pointed to the words. Again, Sophia struggled to read them, but she was thrust back into her body.

Doctor Myers began removing the needles. "How do you feel?"

Sophia opened her eyes. "Amazing. I went somewhere and I was greeted by the same beautiful woman in my dreams. Who is she?"

Doctor Myers smiled. "All will be revealed in good time. Please come into my office. I'd like to give you a list of things that will help you."

Sophia slipped on her socks and shoes, fastened her silver watchband, and slid the bracelet over her wrist. When entered the office, Doctor Myers handed her several sheets of paper. "This is a list of herbs I feel you should start with. If you are still in Sedona next month, I'd like to see you again. I suggest you purchase this book." She held up the thick purple book. "Read all about your body type. The book will suggest types of foods better suited toward your digestive system. It will explain how to put on weight healthily. I do have one piece of advice."

"I'm open."

"You need to create healthy boundaries. You need to stand up for yourself and tell others when enough is enough. Trust in the universe. The laws of karma will be enforced to those who have harmed you in the past." She smiled gently. "It has been a pleasure, Sophia. You are on the right track."

As Sophia left the office, her arms filled with herbs and books, she wondered how the doctor knew she had issues with boundaries. *Who was the beautiful woman dressed in the white flowing gown?*

"Today's hike is short," Cassandra said. They were sitting at the table eating breakfast. The day was warm and sunny.

"I didn't think I had to hike for a few days." Sophia had been focusing on her art work, yoga, and eating correctly. At the moment, she didn't think she could add one more thing to her plate.

"This hike is only a two mile loop. You'll see spectacular red rock views," Cassandra said as she handed her the map with the trail highlighted.

"And I have to go right now?"

"Trust in the universe." Cassandra hugged her. "I'm going to the market. Can I get you anything?"

* * *

Sophia parked her car at the trail head and headed up the path. It was lonely, but, being the only hiker on the trail, she found the solitude gratifying. Walking quickly, without taking in the surrounding scenery, her mind wandered to her children. It was hard after twenty-one years of parenting to be without a job. After all those years of having them underfoot, she was rather attached to them. During the last phone conversation she had had with Ben, he mentioned that he wasn't coming home this summer. He planned to stay in Boulder with his roommates. She sniffled. She was going to miss him. Ben was the one who cleared the table without being asked, mowed the lawn, and still kissed her goodnight. He was her joy and blessing.

Katie was a different story. Looking back, it seemed as if Katie felt she always had to correct her about something. It started when she showed up to the mother/daughter tea dressed in jeans and a tee-shirt. All the other mothers had worn dresses or pressed pants and starched shirts, their faces expertly made-up. Now Katie was trying to convince Sophia to fight for Brad—not to give in and let Leslie have him. Sophia tried to explain that even if he came crawling back on his hands and knees, she wouldn't take him back. It was over. But Katie couldn't accept it. Her latest idea was for Sophia to go to one of those fancy spas and have a complete make-over, then fly home and seduce him.

She felt a tear wanting to form as she thought about her daughter. Even though they often were at odds with each other, she missed her desperately and had been depressed for months after she left for college. She remembered sitting in Katie's room, staring at her doll collection, the high school memorabilia that littered her book shelves and walls, and the clothes left hanging in the closet. A chapter in her life had ended.

Sophia turned the corner and immediately stopped when she saw a deer standing in the path, munching on a bush. She had never been this close to a deer. Would it bite? The deer stopped eating, then transformed into a stunning woman with golden hair dressed in a blue robe. "Ah, Sophia" the woman said. "I have been waiting for you."

One would think by now that she would be used to animals changing into humans, but she wasn't. She clutched her heart. "Who are you?"

The woman smiled. "I am Demeter, the goddess of harvest. I offer solace to mothers struggling with separation from their children. I'm sure you've heard my story. My daughter, Persephone, was abducted by Hades to become his bride. I never did like that man. I didn't think he was good enough for my daughter." She grinned. "Mothers never do, you know. But Zeus had a level head, and we struck a deal."

Sophia racked her brain as she tried to remember the myth she had read during her freshman year in college. "Yes. I remember that story, but I always thought it was just a story."

Demeter smiled. "All stories come from somewhere, my dear. They are someone's truth. I realize how saddened you are by the events in your life. Your family is split apart. Your children are growing away from you. We mothers create and nurture life. It's hard for mothers to realize that the act of giving birth begins a child's separation from the mother. You need to work through your sorrow."

Even though she nodded in agreement, she still felt sad. Ben wasn't coming home, and Katie was trying to talk Brad into letting her go to Europe with several of her friends for the summer. Sophia didn't know where Brad would get the money. Rape some client with his large billable hours; take a second on Leslie's ring? But Katie was on academic probation at the moment, and Sophia didn't think she should go anywhere but summer school. She wanted to call him and tell him he was out of his mind for even listening to her request, but she was forbidden by her lawyer to contact him. "You're right. I know I need to let go."

"You are the mother of adult children, even if you think they don't act like adults." Demeter shook her head. "I had that problem with Persephone until she was about thirty." *Shit! Katie is only eighteen. It sounds like a death-sentence.*

"You need to craft a new life, Sophia. Your marriage is over and your children are grown. Create a new relationship with your children so you can get on with the business of living. There are many times I am envious of those still in the human form."

Sophia sat on the rock and stared at the woman, realizing that parenting, like life, wasn't a race she was going to win. She needed to learn how to lose with grace, so her children and grandchildren would come and see her when she was bent over with age. In fact, the more she thought about it, the more she realized that she wanted grace more than anything in her life. Grace to let life flow through her, grace to accept where she was, and grace to embrace her new opportunities.

"What do I do now?"

Demeter leaned over and kissed her on the cheek. "You will be tested shortly. Resist the temptation to rush in and fix it."

"Fix what?" *I'm not good at fixing anything. Look at my life.*

"All will be revealed in good time. Stay resourceful, flexible, connected, and true. Just go down the road a piece and turn left at the large boulder." Suddenly the dirt swirled around her. Sophia closed her eyes and when she opened them the woman was gone. The deer continued to munch on the leaves and Sophia no longer feared the beautiful animal.

Chapter 12

It was a bright, warm day with the temperature pushing eighty degrees, one of those days when children rode their bikes, couples strolled hand in hand, and you could hear the sound of the backyard grills ignite. The sky was brilliant blue with thick, puffy clouds hovering over the Red Rocks. Cassandra and Dave drove into Phoenix for an appointment with a gallery owner. Sophia felt the tug of the ripening earth, so she drove to the nursery, loaded the wagon with flats of brightly colored annuals and perennials and hurried home with her cache. After unloading the car, she changed into a pair of torn khakis, a bleached tee-shirt, and an old sweatshirt, and rummaged around Cassandra's garage, unearthing a trowel, hoe, and rake. Sticking the trowel in her back pocket, she gathered the rake and hoe, and headed to the backyard. She raked the dead leaves into piles, took off her sweatshirt, and rolled up her sleeves. The warmth of the sun felt marvelous as she allowed her thoughts to drift as she worked with deliberate motions. She set the plants in the soil and watered generously. When she finished, she sat on the porch and admired her work. Her cell phone rang. "Hello."

"Mom? Is that you?"

Her knees quivered. Ben sounded strange. "What's wrong?"

His heavy breathing was obvious. "I'm in trouble."

"What kind of trouble?"

"I'm in jail. I need you to post bail for me."

Her heart stopped. *What was he doing in jail? He had never even gotten a traffic ticket.* "Bail for what?"

"It's … it's a long story."

She shook her head, closed her eyes for a moment and tried to remain calm. "You expect me to post bail, and you're not going to tell me why."

He sighed. "This was a mistake. I should call Dad."

She tried again. "What did you do, Ben?" A litany of horrors circled her brain. He had shoplifted, stolen a car, robbed a bank.

"I got caught selling pot."

"Drugs! You hate drugs. You've always said that people who do drugs are losers."

He stammered. "I was selling to make ends meet, Mom. The cost of living is high here."

"You couldn't get a job waiting tables or mowing lawns? You didn't try getting a job on campus? Your idea of solving the problem is to do something illegal?"

"It was a mistake to call you."

"Are you using?"

"Not that much."

His voice sounded faraway, as if he was in some distant galaxy standing at a payphone staring at Earth. "I raised you better that, Ben."

"Mom, they booked me late last night. This is my one phone call. Please help me."

"There's a commuter flight scheduled to Boulder this afternoon at one thirty-two," the woman said. "There're still several vacant seats."

"I'll take one." Sophia recited her MasterCard number, then hurried into the house, showered, packed a small overnight bag, and left her aunt a note. She was going to fly to Boulder, bail her son out, and spend the night so she could talk some sense into him. Her stomach was churning. She had had a feeling things weren't right with Ben. Lately, on the phone he had seemed distant and once even mentioned that he was struggling with his classes, and that wasn't like him.

The flight was bumpy; the wind bounced the small jet between the mountains like a ping-pong ball. She held on, closed her eyes, and prayed. Had she screwed her children up by running away? God, she felt so guilty. It was all her fault. She should have stayed home. She remembered Demeter's warning of not being co-dependent.

None of this is my fault. I didn't make him smoke pot. Shit. I didn't even smoke pot in the seventies. No, this was all his doing. He has to take responsibility for his actions.

When she arrived in Boulder, the air was cool, so she zipped up her parka and went to find a cab.

"Where to?" the driver asked.

"The county jail."

The man nodded. "Kid in trouble?"

She slid into the backseat. "How did you know?"

"You're not the first parent to fly in to get their kid out of trouble. Don't worry. He'll grow up. Sometimes these things can be a blessing in disguise."

Sophia sank back into the seat. The cab smelled of cigarettes and sweat. She thought she knew her children. Where had she gone wrong? She had majored in Ben and Katie. She knew their favorite foods, TV shows, the music they listened to, the movies they frequented, and their favorite brand of jeans. She had made a career of being their mother, and had showered them with equal dosages of love and affection. Now that she thought about it, she was happy Ben had called her instead of Brad. He would have blamed her, like he blamed her when Katie had gotten caught drinking at the school dance. Their marriage had had two divisions of labor. Brad brought home the paycheck, and she took care of the house and the children.

The cab pulled up in front of a two-story beige building. "That'll be ten-forty," the man said.

She handed him twenty dollars. "Thank you. Will you wait for me? I need to find a motel after I get my son out of here."

The man smiled. "Sure. Don't worry, lady." It's going to be okay.

She nodded, forcing back the tears, and entered the building. Nothing in her mommy-career had prepared her for this. A bored-looking man with greasy, graying brown hair stood behind the counter. He glanced up. "May I help you?"

"I'm Sophia Roberts. I'm here to post bail for my son, Ben Roberts."

"Ben Roberts," the man echoed. "Let me find his paperwork." He dug through a thick stack, pulled out several sheets, and bit his lip. "Bail is set for two thousand." He glanced up. "We take MasterCard, Visa, Discover, and of course, cash." She handed her card to the man.

"Just give me a few minutes to process his paperwork. He will need to show up tomorrow morning at ten to see the judge."

Sophia nodded, feeling sick to her stomach, and took the vacant seat next to a tall, thin man. He nodded at her, then continued reading the newspaper. She stared at the bland walls and waited. How did she get here? Wasn't she just driving the car pool and waiting at the dentist's office? Didn't she just stay up late baking cookies for his track team? A deputy finally led Ben out. She barely recognized her son. The same little boy she had loved and cared for, made sure he took his vitamins, went to bed on time, and ate healthy meals seemed to have lost twenty pounds. His sandy blond hair was dirty and reached down to his thin shoulders. His blue eyes looked sad and haunted. He wrapped his arms around her neck and hugged her. "Thanks, Mom." She forced the tears back as she hugged him tightly. "Let's get out of here," he whispered.

She thanked the deputy and escorted Ben to the waiting cab. The driver opened the door. "There's a nice motel a couple of miles away. It has a restaurant."

"That will be great," she said. "Thank you."

She turned to Ben. "You have to see the judge in the morning. Are you going to miss any classes?"

"I don't have class until two."

Mother and son were silent on the short ride. Sophia paid the man, thanked him for his help, and went to the motel office. "I need a room for one night," she told the elderly clerk. "Two double beds, please."

As soon as they entered the room she threw her bag down on the bed. "Is there someone you can call who'll bring you a change of clothes?"

"Why don't I just go back to my place? You can pick me up in the morning."

She stared at him and decided he must be on drugs because he wasn't thinking clearly. "I just put up money I don't have. I want to make sure you'll visit the judge in the morning. You need to be with me right now."

He shrugged. "Whatever." He picked up the phone, dialed, and spoke in a low voice. When he finished, he turned to her. "Drew will be over in a few with some of my things. I'm sorry, Mom. I know you're disappointed."

"I don't know what to think, Ben. Where did I go wrong? Selling drugs? And look at you. You look awful. It looks to me like you're using something else besides pot."

He averted her eyes. "It's nothing you did. I made the decision. I'm sorry I disappointed you. You're not going to tell Dad?"

She remembered Brad's volatile temper. "I'm not going to say anything now, but you're going to have to get some help." She reached into her bag and pulled out her shampoo and conditioner. "Here, take a shower. You need it."

Catherine MacDonald

He emerged from the shower, clean and scrubbed, wearing the clothes his roommate had dropped off. His pants hung around his thin hips. She had ordered pizza, chicken wings, sodas, and a salad from the restaurant and arranged it on the circular table in the corner. "Why don't we eat? Then we can get some sleep. We'll talk tomorrow when you're rested."

He nodded, as if she had granted him a stay of execution. He sat, took a slice of pizza, and gobbled it down in two bites. He devoured the chicken wings, drank two sodas, and reached for another slice of pizza. Sophia nibbled on the salad and picked at a slice of pizza as she watched him eat. *This looks like Ben*, she thought, watching him reach for the rest of the chicken wings. When he had been in high school, she could barely keep the refrigerator filled. He pushed his plate back. "Thanks, Mom. That was delicious and I'm full."

"Why don't you brush your teeth and climb into bed. We can watch whatever you want on the tube." She handed him a new toothbrush. As he excused himself and went to the bathroom, she wondered if the pot had stained his teeth. She had always made sure that he had visited the dentist twice a year. After he had had his braces removed, she had his teeth professionally bleached.

He returned, smiled sheepishly, climbed into bed, and reached for the remote. He channel surfed, finally decided on a movie, and stared blankly at the screen. She cleaned up the mess and prepared for bed. It had been a long day.

Tossing and turning that night, the stiff cotton sheets twisting around her legs, Sophia finally fell asleep. In her dream, she was walking along the beach, the waves lapping gently at her feet. A distinguished woman dressed in a flowing pink and white robe appeared. The woman smiled serenely and bowed. "I am Kuan Yin. I am here to give you strength and compassion as you deal with the people who have brought you tribulation." She held out her hands and Sophia grasped them. "I have taken a vow to love mankind. I appear to you here, and not in the Red Rocks, because I hear the cry of your soul. My compassion will flood your soul whenever you call me. Your assignment is to manifest compassion to those who have hurt you deeply."

Sophia gazed into the woman's eyes and saw unconditional love. She nodded. "I understand why you are here. I need to forgive my son and my husband. I'm trying, but it's hard. I'm so angry."

The woman nodded. "That is to be expected. It is not a sin to be angry with someone you love. It reminds you that you are human and struggling to be divine. Your husband wronged you. Forgive him so you can go forward. Your anger stalls your path. But never forget what he did. Your son is a different matter. He is young and still needs your guidance. Don't chastise yourself for his mistakes. You are not responsible for your children's mistakes. The lessons are theirs to learn. You must learn to detach and let them make their own mistakes. That is the only way they will learn. Your job is to listen and give wise counsel if asked." Her face grew somber. "Your daughter will cause you concern soon." The woman leaned over and kissed her gently on the forehead and then vanished as quickly as she had appeared.

Ben stood and listened while the judge read the charges. "Do you have anything to say for yourself?" he asked.

"No, your honor. I am guilty."

The judge studied Ben. "This is your first offense. I have your school transcript. Until this semester, you were a top student. It appears you've made some poor choices. Do you realize the seriousness of your crime?"

Ben bowed his head in shame. "Yes, sir. I promise I will never use or sell drugs again."

"I could sentence you to a year in jail," the judge said. "I have put other young men and women away for similar crimes." He paused. "However, I am not going to do that." Ben's eyes widened. Earlier that morning she and Ben had talked about what they would do if he was convicted. "I see a young man standing before me with great potential. You're smart, a good student, and you have a caring parent. I don't understand why you would use drugs."

Ben shrugged. "I don't know either, sir. It was a stupid thing for me to do."

"Yes, it was," the judge said, looking Ben straight in the eye. "I sentence you to a drug program. You will be tested at their will. You will complete one hundred hours of community service. After your semester ends, you will return home to your mother. She will keep in contact with me. You will keep clean, get a job, and do what she says. Is that clear?"

Ben's eyes widened. "I don't have to go to jail?"

The judge glanced at Sophia. "No, not unless you break the rules I have laid out for you. Is that acceptable to you, Mrs. Roberts?"

"Yes, your honor," she said. She didn't want to tell her son or the judge that she had no home. She had no source of income, and she was currently on some journey to release her divine diva. She nodded. "That will be fine."

The judge banged his gavel on the desk. "You're dismissed. Next case."

Ben and Sophia walked back to the motel, each silent with their own thoughts. Drugs, she thought. It didn't make sense. He had been so adamant against them in high school, calling the kids who did drugs losers and leeches on society. Had she loved her children too much? But she remembered the advice imparted by the woman in her dream and thought about the humor of the universe. Last fall she had been despondent because she thought her mommy job was over, and now the universe had dropped her son with all his problems into her lap. She remembered the woman's warning about Katie. "When's school out?"

"May twenty-eighth. Are you moving back into the house?"

"Your dad's selling it," Sophia said. "I don't know what I'm going to do, but I'll be back in town by then." She started to explain the journey she was on, but quickly decided against it. Ben had enough issues right now, without her adding her own troubles to the mix. "It's April fourteenth. That gives me five weeks to finish what I'm doing in Sedona. I'll be back by the time you're out of school. I'll find a condo or an apartment." She laughed. "You won't be the only one looking for a job, too."

He stopped and stared at her. "Don't you think you should do something with your art? You were always so talented, Mom. I remember when I was in grade school and all the things you did for my teachers. I loved it when you came into the classroom and taught the art lessons. Maybe you could get a job at the museum or teach art."

Sophia nodded. "Those are good ideas. I'll have to think about them. Obviously, I'm going to have to find something that will pay the bills." She glanced at her watch. "My flight leaves in two hours. It's almost noon. Don't you have class soon?"

"Yes, but I haven't done my work. I don't know if I want to continue with school. I've been thinking of taking a year off. I could work at one of the ski resorts and earn some money."

"But after this year you only have one year left. Why would you quit when you're so close to finishing?"

"I don't like my major, Mom. Dad picked it, remember?"

Sophia remembered Brad's lectures at the dinner table. Ben was going to be a lawyer and join him in the firm. They would be a father/son team. "You don't have to be a lawyer if you don't want to. You can be anything you want."

"What else can I do with a political science major?"

"I don't know, but I'm sure you'll think of something. You need to finish college, because it will open doors for you. It shows a potential employer that you are trainable and can complete a task."

"I'll think about it, but I don't want to be a lawyer."

She remembered the countless cocktail parties she and Brad had attended with the other lawyers from his firm. Their main goal was to see how much money they could bill their clients, not the good they could do or the services they would perform. "Something will develop. You have your entire life before you. Ben, promise me you'll stay away from drugs."

"I promise, Mom. I've learned my lesson. I never want to spend another night in jail."

Ben's roommate, a thin young man with a black goatee and several silver earrings in his ears, drove her to the airport. "Thank you, Drew. It was nice meeting you."

"Have a good flight, Mrs. Roberts," Drew said.

Sophia kissed Ben. "I will see you back in Reno in six weeks. I'll check in on you periodically. Make sure you attend classes, start your community service, and complete the drug program."

"I'm sorry to drag you into this, Mom," Ben said. "I know you're having a difficult time yourself. I didn't mean to add to it."

Sophia hugged him tightly, picked up her bag, and went through security. When she was aboard the commuter plane, she strapped herself in and closed her eyes. The tiny jet taxied to the end of the runway and took its place in the long line. When it finally crept its way to the front of the line, the pilot gunned the engines and raced the plane down the runway. Feeling light-headed as the plane lifted off, she gripped the arm rests and stared out the window at the Rocky Mountains. The rough air battered the tiny jet. Back and forth. Back and forth. She closed her eyes and made the sign of the cross. Old habits are hard to break. The captain's soft voice was barely audible as he assured the passengers over the loudspeaker that everything was okay, just normal mountain turbulence. "Keep your seatbelts securely fastened," he advised.

She tugged at hers as she realized that the flimsy lap belt would do nothing to protect her if the plane suddenly lunged out of the sky and spiraled towards earth like a meteor.

Chapter 13

As the plane circled the landing field, Sophia spied the trail where she had met the first diva. *What was her name again? That's right. White Buffalo Woman.* Twisting the tissue in her hand and remembering the rabbit who suddenly transformed into a beautiful woman, she recounted her journey and the tasks given. First there had been Ruby, the gatekeeper, then White Buffalo woman, who told her to release her martyr energy. That had been difficult. Catholicism and martyrdom went together like spaghetti and meatballs. Next, she had met the apparition in the church who convinced her to forgive the priest, followed by the old woman with three faces. *What was her name?* Hecate, that's it. She was old and ugly, but she had persuaded her to confront Brad about his abuse. Then there was Demeter, who told her not to be co-dependant. Had she really been co-dependant? She sighed. *Yes.* She had always worried about what others thought. She shivered as she remembered her dream the night before and the woman who told her to use compassion as she dealt with her son. She had wanted to strangle Ben. Drugs! A National Merit Scholar busted for pot.

The plane landed abruptly and taxied to the gate. She grabbed her overnight bag and stepped out into the warm air. Cassandra stood behind the chain link fence waving. "Is he okay?"

"Yes. He's lucky the judge didn't throw the book at him. I'm still in shock."

Cassandra wrapped her arm around her. "I don't understand kids today. Why would they want to do drugs when the world is so beautiful?"

"Maybe Ben's world isn't that beautiful," Sophia said softly. She explained the judge's conditions.

"Do you think it's wise to go back to Reno?"

"I don't know. It looks like I'm going to have to go home and find a job and a place to live, but let's not talk about it now. I'm tired."

Cassandra smiled. "Come along. Dave's made vegetarian lasagna for dinner. You must be famished from your trip." She led Sophia to the car and drove home.

At dinner that evening, Dave and Cassandra discussed Cassandra's up-coming art show, local politics and the weather, while Sophia picked at her food. She really didn't feel like eating, even though the lasagna was delicious, and she didn't feel like small talk either. She pushed her plate away. "I'm going to bed. I need to do some thinking."

Her aunt nodded. "You look tired, honey. Ben's going to be okay. I promise."

Sophia leaned over and kissed her aunt and Dave. "Thanks for dinner. Sorry I didn't eat more. I'll feel better in the morning." She was concerned about Katie, but didn't want to tell her aunt the woman's prediction. She called her daughter, but Katie didn't answer her cell phone, next tried the dorm room, but only the answering machine answered.

Sophia felt her pants tighten around her waist and realized that the three healthy meals and two snacks a day Cassandra was forcing her to eat was showing. She stood in front of the mirror, turned sideways and glanced at her behind. "You're looking wonderful," Cassandra said, coming up behind her.

"Am I fat?" Sophia asked.

Her aunt grinned. "You look juicy. Look in the mirror and tell me what you see."

Sophia stared at her reflection. A woman of indeterminable age stared back. Her cheeks were rosy, her blue eyes sparkled, and her complexion glowed.

"You look absolutely beautiful," Cassandra said. "Alive and juicy. Look at the energy that emits from your crown."

Sophia studied her reflection. It was as if there were rays of light beaming from her head in all directions. "What's happened to me?"

Cassandra grinned and hugged her. "You are activating your divine diva who has been slumbering in your soul. I think it's time for Cathedral Rock."

"You mentioned that was a difficult hike," she argued. "I don't think I'm in good enough shape yet."

"Nonsense. You're ready. Besides, we have to step up our program if you're leaving in four weeks. You'll start out first thing in the morning. Meanwhile, the studio's free right now. Why don't you go and play?"

Sophia went to the studio. She played with the paints, tried her hand at the pottery wheel, but nothing emerged. Several hours later she heard a knock at the door.

"How are you doing?" her aunt asked as she entered the room.

Sophia gazed up from a watercolor she was working on. "I don't know what's wrong with me today. Nothing's flowing. Look at the colors. They've run together. The picture doesn't have any energy."

Her aunt studied the painting. "It has possibilities, but that's not the point. You need to understand that in the creative process one has to be willing to make mistakes. Creating is hard work. There will be days when the flow isn't there, but that is all part of the process. The artist has to be willing to take risks and to make mistakes." She laughed. "That's the problem with most people. They assume that creating art is easy. When they encounter an obstacle, they stop and give up. How many people do you know who have unfinished manuscripts or paintings in their closet?"

Sophia thought for a moment and remembered several people who had written books, but were too scared to let anyone read them, and a couple of women who had hidden their paintings in the back of their closets. "So what do I do?"

"You never give up. You realize that along with the great art comes the mundane. It is working through the mundane that gets the artist to greatness. When you examine the work of a master, don't assume that it flowed easily. You need to understand the enormous effort that went into that work of art, the many drafts, the sketches thrown in the wastebasket, the clay wadded up and stuck back in the bucket. The artist has to continually challenge himself or herself to stay on task, to show up on the page, the canvas, or the wheel. That discipline is what will separate you from the others."

Sophia set her brush down. "It just gets so frustrating. There are days when I feel the flow and then there are days like today. Nothing will come out that's any good."

Cassandra smiled gently. "I learned this many years ago from a wise man. If something is worth doing, it's worth doing poorly. You are going to have shitty paintings or drawings to get to the really good stuff." She stroked Sophia's cheek. "Let's go into my sanctuary so I can attune you. You're still out of balance."

Sophia giggled. "Attune me? Am I a piano?"

"No. I'm just going to open up your chakras and send some energy."

Sophia gasped. "What are my chakras?" Her mind swirled as she studied her aunt.

"Chakras are invisible energy centers that we all have. Your body contains seven chakras. This won't hurt you," her aunt reassured. "It'll help. I promise." She followed her aunt into the sanctuary. "Sit on that pillow," Cassandra said. "I'm going to light a candle." She followed instructions, sat on the pillow, and allowed her body to relax.

"Close your eyes," Cassandra said. "Become aware of your breath. Inhale and count to six, then exhale and count to six. Then start over again. If thoughts float into your mind, don't attach to them, just let them float away. Stay in the present moment." Sophia felt her aunt wave her hands over her head and chant unfamiliar words as she picked up Sophia's hands and drew strange symbols in her palms. Sophia struggled to keep her eyes closed, but she was interested in what her aunt was doing, so every few minutes she would open them and peek.

"Imagine the most peaceful, safe, beautiful and magical garden," Cassandra said. "This is your own personal space. No one can enter. Notice the flowers, the color of the sky, and the landscape. Smell the green plants." Sophia inhaled and exhaled. "Hear the sound of the wind rustling through the trees and the soothing songs of the birds. Do you feel happy and peaceful?" Sophia nodded. She felt blissful. "Good," her aunt said. "This is the space you need to visit every time you find yourself stuck. Do you see a figure approaching."

Sophia smiled as she recognized the beautiful woman dressed in the long flowing white gown. The woman's face lingered in front of her, looking alive and full of love.

"She is always here to help you," Cassandra said softly. "Ask her what you can do to help yourself and your art. Listen carefully to the sound of her voice as she tells you exactly what you need to do right now. Listen carefully and don't edit what you hear. Trust her. She knows what's best for you. Realize that you have the power to change your life. Know that you will create the art you need to bring into the world and become a vortex for that creative energy."

Sophia started to ask the woman in the flowing white gown who she was, but the woman vanished.

That night Sophia's dreams were dramatic. At one point she found herself in an open sunny meadow lying on an operating table. Women dressed in long flowing purple gowns surrounded her, chanting unfamiliar words. One woman held a shaft of sunlight over Sophia's chest and drove the shaft downward toward her heart. She felt warm pressure enter her chest and caress her heart. The woman withdrew the shaft and smiled broadly at the other women. "No further surgery needed."

The women clapped and cheered.

* * *

Sophia hiked the steep trail toward Cathedral Rock, her feet slipping on the rocks. The trail was strenuous. She stopped several times to catch her breath and even thought about abandoning the hike, telling her aunt she had made it, and concocting some vision she had seen.

"You're almost to the top," a male voice said. She glanced up. A man hiked toward her. "Don't stop now," he said. "You'll lose your momentum."

Sophia stopped and leaned on a boulder. "How much farther?" She observed the man coming towards her. He was tall with sandy blond hair, a blond mustache, and long tanned muscular legs. He was somewhere in his late thirties or early forties. He smiled and her heart skipped a beat. He was cute.

"About a half a mile," the man said. He stopped and smiled. "You'll make it. Just remember, it's one foot in front of the other. I haven't seen you around here before. Are you visiting?"

"Yes. I'm staying with my aunt. I came to Sedona to…" She paused. "You don't want to hear about my problems. I'm Sophia."

The man grinned, reached for his water bottle and took a drink. "Ah, Sophia, the goddess of wisdom. I'm Kurt Brown. I'm a massage therapist in town. If you need a massage after your hike, I'd be happy to oblige."

She thought about his large capable hands caressing her body and smiled. "Do you have a card?"

Kurt reached into his pocket and let out a broad grin. "I just happen to carry them for situations like this." As she took the card from him, her hand gently brushed his, and she felt a wave of energy. She jumped back. "That was electrifying," he said.

Sophia smiled and tried to regain her composure. She was a grown woman, and her knees wobbled like jelly. His piercing gaze almost made her feel uncomfortable. It was as if she knew him from somewhere, but that wasn't possible. "I better finish this hike," she said.

"Would you care to meet for a drink this evening?" Kurt asked.

"I don't think that's a good idea."

"I'm not going to attack you. We could meet in the afternoon. Just friends," he said. "I'd like to get to know you."

"I'm a little bit older than you," she said.

"I've always had a thing for older women," he teased. "I won't bite, I promise. Call me if you feel like chatting with a friend. Enjoy your hike." He smiled and took off down the hill.

Sophia watched as he hiked down the trail. God, he was good looking, but she didn't need to complicate her life right now. He had to be at least ten years younger. *What would they talk about?*

Gasping for breath and wondering what was so important about this hike, she continued up the rocky trail. The day was warm. The temperature had to be over eighty and there wasn't a cloud in the sky. Sophia slipped on the rocks, banged her knee, and cursed her aunt. *Why do I have to do this? Haven't I had enough lessons? How am I supposed to remember all this?*

After an hour of climbing the rocky terrain, Sophia finally made it to the top, paused and surveyed her surroundings. Large dramatic rocks, no vegetation, and there wasn't a soul around. She gazed down the mountain and felt nauseous. *I hate heights* she thought as she sat on a large red rock and took out her water bottle.

Sophia took several big sips. *Now what? I can't imagine an animal appearing to me up here.* As she inhaled the thin air, she felt a current of energy, so she closed her eyes and leaned back against the boulder. Suddenly she heard the rustling of leaves, which was strange, because there were no trees. Next she heard the sounds of flutes. *This is strange*, she thought as she opened her eyes and gasped. A swarm of birds hovered above her.

"Do not be afraid," one of the birds said. "We are here to guide you." The birds suddenly transformed into nine beautiful women playing harps. "We are the muses. We've been sent to inspire you and help you tap into your well of creativity. Your spirit has been smothered for too long. You are ripe with possibilities."

Sophia stared at the beautiful women and felt a flood tide of raw energy. A tall muse with flowing brown hair smiled. "We have been sent to remind you that being creative is part of being human."

A shorter muse spoke. "You have the makings of a great artist, Sophia. The world needs your vision."

"You have been walking on the earth on auto pilot," a muse with curly red hair said. "Clarity of mind, body, and spirit is the key to creativity. When the artist in you is alive, you become enthused with spirit."

"Art is an act of faith," another muse said.

Sophia felt confused. "What am I supposed to do?"

"Show up and pay attention," said the muse with the long silver hair. "You have stifled your creativity. Your job as an artist is to make something new, something the world has not seen before. It is your primary job to listen to the inspiration we will whisper and observe the beauty of the world. To move into a creative relationship with us, all you need to do is create. The power of creation comes through your senses. We are always with you. Call for us. We will help you."

"You have also been chosen as the messenger," the youngest muse added. "When the time is right, the message will be delivered."

"The messenger for what?" she asked. This hike was becoming more bizarre than the others.

"All will be revealed in good time," said the muse with the flowing blond hair.

"Okay," she said. "I will be patient, but could you clear something up for me." The muses smiled. "If I need inspiration, all I need to do is call for you, and you'll be there?"

"That's all there is to it," said the muse with the red hair. "Creativity is ever-flowing from the Goddess. You cannot hold it in, or you will suffer. Your assignment is to show the world what's in your heart."

What was really in her heart? She started to ask the muses, but they picked up their harps and began playing. The music became louder as the muses faded from sight.

"Remember, Sophia. We are always with you. Stay resourceful, flexible, connected, and true. Just go down the trail a piece. Turn left at the large boulder. It is a faster route back down the mountain."

Chapter 14

Sophia fingered the business card and stared at his name. Should she call him? Maybe he was just being nice. Why was he interested in her? She was older than him. Maybe there was something wrong with him. God, he was cute. She picked up the phone, started to dial, then set it the phone back in the cradle. She was fifty—not fifteen. But she gathered a bit more courage and did dial the number this time. He answered in the third ring. "Kurt, it's Sophia. I met you on the trail this morning."

"Ah, Sophia. I was hoping you'd call. I see you made it down the mountain in one piece."

"That was a difficult hike, but I'm glad I did it."

"Can I interest you in a massage?" he asked.

"How about if we meet for some iced tea? Say four o'clock at Coyote Moon."

"I have a three-thirty massage appointment. Could we say closer to five?"

"Five would be fine. I'll see you then."

"I look forward to it, Sophia." He hung up.

She leaned against the counter. She felt giddy, like a teenager. Having several hours to spare before meeting Kurt and wanting to do something productive, she went to find her aunt.

Sophia found Cassandra, where she expected, in the studio working on her painting. "Making art is a spiritual practice," Cassandra explained. "You can talk directly to the source by working with your hands and mind. The creative process is attached to the deepest part of your soul."

Sophia glanced up from the watercolor she had been working on. "I'm beginning to understand. It's as if a divine presence takes over my hand."

"And time seems to melt away," Cassandra added.

"Yes, you're right. Hours go by and it feels like minutes." Sophia glanced at her watch. It was three-thirty already and she was meeting Kurt soon. Would he stand her up? She remembered a shy boy from a frat house who asked her to a dance, then never showed up for their date.

Cassandra leaned over her work. "Your colors are amazing. That's Cathedral Rock."

Sophia beamed. "I just started playing with the washes and magic appeared." She leaned back and admired her work. *Not bad*. The picture really did look like the rock she had just climbed. Lately she had been painting a lot, often taking her work out into the brilliant landscape of the Red Rocks.

"Your paintings are magnificent," Cassandra said, wiping pain from her hands, then pointing to a collection by the window. "I'm having a show next week at the Aztec Gallery. Maybe it's time we show some of your work."

Sophia gasped. "I'm not ready. My work is too primitive."

"Far from it, my dear. Your work is like a beautiful bird that has been let out of its cage. It's ready for the world to see."

"You mean to be judged." She shook her head, indicating that she did not agree with Cassandra's suggestion. "I'm not strong enough."

Cassandra smiled gently. "Do you understand who critics really are?"

"Sure," she said. "They are people who have studied art and have degrees."

Her aunt laughed. "That's true. Some of them are, but I have a different definition."

"And what's that?" She remembered an art teacher in college who told her that she had no talent and should choose elementary education as a major.

"I believe critics are frustrated artists. They're not brave enough to put their art out into the world, or they didn't practice enough, so they spend their energy ripping up other people's creations and damaging their souls."

Sophia rinsed her paint brush in a jar of cool water, then she massaged it on a bar of soap to remove the remaining paint. She thought about what Cassandra had said while she shaped the brush back to its natural point. "That does make sense when you present it that way. I always thought critics were the gods of the art world."

"Well, they want you to think that way. I wonder how many fragile spirits they have killed with their flippant comments? Art is the ultimate religious act. There is no way you can do it incorrectly." Cassandra leaned over Sophia. "But for what it's worth, I think you have an innate talent. I remember when you were a little girl and spent hours in your bedroom painting picture after picture. You had talent back then, but your mother didn't want you to follow in our family's footsteps."

"What footsteps? You're the only one I knew who was an artist."

"No, my dear" Cassandra said. "You come from a long line of artists. Your uncle was a painter; your grandfather was a painter, and his father. It runs in your blood."

Sophia thought about it for a moment. "You know, that makes sense. Mother got really upset when I declared art as my major in college. She drove down to school and forced me to change. She said she had seen enough people starve while trying to live the artist's life."

"Your uncle never did sell much. He spent more time with the bottle than the brush, but your grandfather was very talented. He painted on the weekends. He taught me." As she smiled, she looked as if she was a thousand years away. "We would sneak into the shed and play. My mother never approved, and I think your mother was scared of disobeying her. Your mother meant well. She was just trying to protect you. The universe is filled with art, Sophia. Look around you. The Goddess is loving and kind. She only wants the best for all of us. Tomorrow we're taking some of your work to the gallery. You'll like Leila, she's the owner. She'll be honest with you. I promise."

Kurt was sitting at a table in the corner when Sophia arrived. She hurried over. "I'm sorry I'm late." He stood and pulled out the chair for her. *Oh, my God, a gentleman.* Brad had never pulled out the chair. She smiled at him. He was gorgeous. What did he see in her?

"I'm glad you decided to have tea with me," he said. "I was afraid I came on too strong on the trail."

"No. I was just angry at my aunt for making me take that hike. She's got me following some. . ." She paused. *That's a quick way to lose a guy, Sophia. Tell him you're on some fairy-tale adventure.*

Kurt grinned. His teeth gleamed. "Who is your aunt?"

"Cassandra Wilson." She wondered what he thought of her, or even if he knew her.

Kurt laughed. "Your aunt is great. She comes in several times a year for a massage. She's a fabulous artist. I have several of her pieces." He studied Sophia. "Are you an artist, too?"

Sophia started to say, no. She was a mother who dappled in real estate, and she was so horrible she was fired. She paused. "Well, yes. I paint. Actually, I've painted for years. My husband never approved."

Kurt's eyes widened. "You're married?"

"Actually, I'm going through a divorce. We're fighting over the assets. He's a lawyer."

Kurt smiled. "I'm sorry. I was married to a lawyer once. We divorced about five years ago. No kids. You?"

"Two. Ben's almost twenty-one and Katie turned nineteen in February. They're away at school."

A young waitress came over and took their orders. "Two iced herbal teas," Kurt said. "Do you want anything else?" he asked. She shook her head. She was so nervous in his presence she wasn't sure she could drink the tea without dribbling all over herself. After the waitress left, he leaned across the table. "I think you are a beautiful woman, Sophia. Your husband is a fool to leave you."

"That's the nicest thing anyone has said to me in a long time," she said. "Thank you. Now why don't you tell me about yourself?"

He leaned back in his chair. "Well, I went to college at the University of Arizona, fell in love with the desert, and decided not to return to the east. I grew up in upstate New York, where the winters are long and cold. I studied architecture, went to work for a large firm in Phoenix, but didn't like the corporate mentality. When my wife and I got divorced, I realized there was nothing keeping me in the real world, so I started looking for other options. I took some massage classes at the local junior college and discovered I liked working with my hands on people's bodies. I quit my job, enrolled in a massage school, and started waiting tables at night to pay the bills. I've been practicing massage for two years. I love my work. Recently I've been certified with Reiki, and I use the energy work in my practice now. I'd love to give you a massage. On the house." He let out an almost seductive smile.

The waitress served the tea. Sophia stared at Kurt, imagining his capable hands on her body. "I'd like that, too."

Catherine MacDonald

"I have an opening at three Thursday afternoon," he said. He reached into his pocket and slid a business card across the table. "The address is on the back."

She smiled. "I have your card. Could we make it next week?"

"Next week is fine. Thursday at three?"

She nodded. "That would be wonderful." Could she tone up enough by then? Even though she was slender, her skin still seemed loose.

"Why don't you tell me more about you? Why are you in Sedona?" Kurt asked.

Sophia explained her life in Reno, her children, and the reason she had fled to Sedona. He didn't even look surprised when she confided in him that she was on a journey to find her divine diva. When she told him she had recently turned fifty, he grinned and leaned across the table. "I think older women are sexy. They don't have the head problems the younger women have."

"How old are you, Kurt?"

"Thirty-nine."

"You're not even forty."

"Next December. My wife was eight years older than me."

She laughed. "I guess you do like older women."

"My first crush was on Mrs. Jones. She was my mother's friend." He whistled. "She was spectacular."

They spent the next hour chatting, and by the time Kurt walked her to her car, she was smitten. "I'll see you next Thursday," he said.

She got goose bumps imagining his strong hands working her flesh. "Three o'clock. I'll be there." She wondered how she was going to make it until then.

* * *

"These are breathtaking. Do you have any more?" Leila asked. She was a tall woman, almost six feet, with thick silver hair swept up in a bouffant. She wore a silver and gray caftan and her wrists jangled with multiple silver bracelets.

"There are several more in Cassandra's studio," she said. "Why?"

Leila grinned. "Because I think these will sell." She held up the painting of Cathedral Rock. The tall, craggy rocks touched the impossible blue sky. "You've managed to capture the essence of the Red Rocks. Tourists will snap these up, especially if we price them right."

"How much do you think you can get for one of these?" Cassandra asked.

Leila tilted her head and stroked her chin. "Hmm, unframed, probably one hundred. If I frame it, two twenty-five."

Sophia gasped. "A hundred dollars for one of my paintings!"

"If you were well-known, like your aunt, I could fetch several thousand. But that will come in time, my dear."

Remembering the muses and their prediction, Sophia took a deep breath. "This feels like one of my dreams. I'm afraid if I pinch myself, I'll wake up."

Cassandra leaned over and pinched her. "Did you wake up?"

"No. I'm still standing in this beautiful art gallery." Sophia said, with a look of disbelief still on her face.

"I predict that when your work becomes marketed, your pictures will bring you a handsome sum. Can you produce a few more by next week?"

"I don't see why not. I'm free," Sophia said.

"You still have a couple more hikes," Cassandra mentioned.

"I thought I was done."

Catherine MacDonald

"Almost, then there's your croning ceremony," Cassandra said.

"Ah, so you must have turned fifty," Leila said. "Fifty was a wonderful age for me. I finally felt like I was an adult and finally in charge of my life. My children were grown, and my parents were living the good life in Florida. I still had so much energy and enthusiasm. I hope you invite me, Cassandra. I love these things."

"You'll be first on my list." Cassandra lightly touched her arm. "We need to get going." She kissed Leila on the cheek. "See you soon."

"Thank you, Leila, for giving me a chance," Sophia said. "I hope my work lives up to your expectations."

"Of course it will, my dear. Goddess Bless." Leila led them to the door and escorted them out into the brilliant sunlight.

* * *

"It's Mom, Ben. I'm just calling to see how you're doing with your community service."

"They have me working at a home for disadvantaged kids," Ben said. "I help with homework and play basketball with them."

Sophia leaned against the kitchen counter. "Those kids probably didn't have the advantages you had when you were growing up. It's good for you to see how the other half lives."

"I realize how much you sacrificed for us. Some of these kids have been in foster homes their entire lives." Ben's voice lowered. She could hear the emotion. "I'm sorry I screwed up, Mom. I never meant to hurt you. I'm clean now. I haven't done any drugs or had a drink." He laughed. "You know what the irony of the situation is? I'll be twenty-one in July and the only thing I'll celebrate with is a Coke. That's the drink,

Mom. Not the drug. I know I've disappointed you. Have you told Dad?"

She sighed. "We're in the midst of a pretty nasty divorce, Ben. There are some things he doesn't need to know right now. I feel I've let you and Katie down and I'm obviously a failure at marriage."

"He's the one with the girlfriend," Ben pointed out.

"Thanks. I needed to hear that. Did I tell you about the art show I'm going to be in?" Sophia explained about the gallery, Leila, Cassandra's encouragement, and her nervousness.

"That's awesome, Mom. You were always so artistic. Let me know how you do. If I had some money, I'd buy one of your pictures."

Sophia laughed. "I'll paint you one for free. I've got to go now, sweetheart. Take care and I'll talk to you soon." Hanging up, she hugged her legs and stared out the window. It was dark. Cassandra and Dave had gone to a friend's for dinner. They had asked her to accompany them, but she had feigned a headache. Three was a crowd. The thought of Kurt passed through her mind, but she had put him off until next week and she didn't want to seem too eager. Feeling like a schoolgirl, she counted the days until they would meet.

Her stomach growled. After padding to the kitchen, she scanned the refrigerator and decided on a turkey sandwich, even though she was still haunted with her weight obsession, a bag of chips and topped her meal off with a glass of milk. By weighing herself daily, she had never allowed the scale needle to move over the one-hundred mark. She remembered her strict regimen. Twelve hundred calories a day—that was the number her mother had drilled into her head when she had been growing up. When she thought of all those years she had denied herself, she felt angry at her mother for only focusing on what she looked like, and angry at Brad. He had tried to mold her into his version of the perfect wife. She smiled at all the times she had quietly protested—like the time she wore her Birkenstocks to a formal dinner. She remembered his rage. *Well, now he has Leslie, who seems perfectly willing, to play the role of trophy wife.*

Sophia chewed the sandwich as she thought about the muses and the assignment to paint her vision. Mission accomplished. She had painted the trail up to Cathedral Rock. Along the trail she had painted the animals that had appeared to her, and behind each animal stood a diva. That had been the picture Leila had chosen.

She sipped her milk and finished the sandwich. It felt good to eat. What would her mother say if she saw her eating chips and a sandwich smothered in mayonnaise? She had already gained ten pounds, and she hated to admit it. Cassandra was right—she looked much better. Healthy. Vibrant. Alive.

A vision of her mother flashed in her mind, standing in her kitchen drinking the usual—scotch and water, smoking a cigarette. She tapped her foot while she critiqued. "You shouldn't eat ice cream, Sophia. You need to watch your weight. A woman only eats twelve hundred calories a day. No one will marry a fat girl," her words slurred.

She remembered running from the kitchen and slamming her bedroom door shut. She had flung her body down on the bed, wishing her mother would drop dead from those stupid cigarettes. She didn't care if it was a mortal sin. At that point, hell even seemed better than living with her.

She wondered how much harm she had inflicted on her own children and what had she done to Katie to make her despise her so.

Chapter 15

Cassandra handed Sophia a faded blue knapsack. "Today's hike is a little longer, so I've packed you some food and water. The trail is well-marked. You shouldn't get lost. The first part of the hike will take you around Enchantment Resort. Make sure you follow the signs for Vista Trail. The energy's strongest at *Kachina Woman*."

"What's *Kachina Woman*?" This hike was sounding serious. Sophia reached for another energy bar.

"It's a tall red rock spire. Don't worry, you'll recognize her." Cassandra grinned. "You're going to be in for a pleasant surprise."

"I can't imagine it's going to be any stranger than what I've already experienced." Sophia grabbed the knapsack and flung it on her back. "If I'm not back my dark, please send the forest rangers out for me. I might be dinner for some large animal." Sophia grunted.

Cassandra leaned over and kissed her gently on the forehead. "You'll be protected. You always are. Watch out for the javelinas."

"What's a javelina?"

"They're kind of like a porcupine, but larger, uglier, and they smell. You can't miss them." Cassandra explained the habits of the creature.

Great, Sophia thought as she followed her aunt's directions, heading west on the highway, then turning at Dry Creek Road, continuing until she came to a fork in the road. She glanced at her notes, turned left, and followed the road to a stop sign. She turned right, grateful the road was still paved, followed the wooden signs for the canyon, and pulled into the parking lot.

The day was sunny and warm. She put on a large brimmed hat and reached for her knapsack. She thought it was strange that she was the only one in the parking lot, especially since Cassandra had mentioned how popular the hike was. She followed the well-marked trail through the red terrain, keeping her eyes alert for the javelina. Her aunt had mentioned that these creatures lived in the Red Rock country and fed largely on the prickly pear cactus. During the summer months they fed at night, but they were active during the cooler months. She wiped the perspiration from her brow. Her aunt had also mentioned that the animal didn't see well, but had a highly developed sense of smell and often had an odor themselves.

Keeping her eyes peeled for the ugly animal, she hiked the trail but the only animals out were the birds darting in and out of the trees and an occasional squirrel. A hawk with a red tail flew in circles over the landscape, calling "keer!" She paused on the trail, taking a swig of cool water, and saw the bright yellow blossoms of the prickly pear cactus and prayed there weren't javelinas having lunch. The thought of being chased up a tree by several of the smelly creatures terrified her.

"Calm down, Sophia," she reminded herself. "You're protected. Don't overreact." Pushing the negative thoughts from her consciousness, she continued walking and spied the tall red spire her aunt called *Kachina Woman*. Squinting in the bright sunlight, she studied the figure. The rock really did look like a woman. She continued hiking up the trail, the rhythm of her footsteps calming her fragile nerves. Time fell into a gentle rhythm, the ordinary transformed into the sacred as she awaited her next encounter. The motion of her feet lulled her into a blissful state. There was not another soul on the trail. All of a sudden, there was a strange smell; something she had never smelled before. Pausing on the trail, she glanced around, but there was nothing there. She continued walking, turned the corner and gasped. *Shit!*

The javelina snorted. She screamed, "Now what?" She turned her back to the animal, but it snorted louder.

"Do not be afraid," the javelina said. "I am here to help you." The animal suddenly transformed into a gray-haired woman wearing a purple gown tied with scarlet sashes that made an X design across her chest. She sat on a star wearing a gleaming headband of tiny stars and held a jeweled scepter. Beckoning Sophia to take her hand, she said gently, "Do not be afraid. I am Sophia, too, your namesake. Shall we take a little journey?"

Sophia bowed as she realized she was in the presence of someone holy. She clutched the woman's cool hand as they soared into the heavens. As they flew across the sky, scenes from her life passed in vivid color, former conversations were in surround-sound. She saw herself as a child, a teenager, a young wife and mother. She saw herself digging in her garden, driving her children to school, ball games, and dance lessons. She watched her struggles with food, feeling the tears flood her eyes as she recalled denying herself basic nutrition, while her mother stood on the side criticizing her every bite.

As the white light surrounded her, she watched her marriage slowly disintegrate, realizing that the actual decay had taken years. She realized she had to let Brad go gracefully and proceed with her life. That was the only way to heal. She didn't want to be one of those women who carried their divorce around like a heavy suitcase. She glanced at the woman, who continued to hold her hand. They flew into a lush tropical world at the base of a large mountain. The woman clapped and they were whisked up the mountain on the wings of a dove. A large gleaming mansion stood. "Welcome home, my dear. This is where your soul dwells."

Sophia inhaled, breathing in the thick scent of jasmine. If this was where her soul dwelled, she wanted to stay forever. She felt like she was floating in a universe filled with love.

The woman gazed lovingly into her eyes. "You are the wise woman now, Sophia. You have released your divine diva. I granted your life review to illustrate the fact that you have been a wonderful mother, a dutiful daughter, and a good wife. Your difficulty with anorexia and organized religion was your karma. They were lessons from another life you had to learn. Your mother and the Church were the vehicles your soul chose to learn the lessons from. Your difficulty with your husband is another lesson. You need to let go. He has lessons to learn and issues he needs to work on. Let him figure it out for himself. I am pleased with your progress. You have learned that you can never possess another person. Most of your planet is still working on that issue." She shook her head sadly. "Too many people running around trying to control others and the environment. Such a shame."

When the woman smiled, her eyes radiated a love so complete that Sophia felt her soul stir. "A diva is not a noun or an image of art," the woman said. "A diva is a verb, moving and doing, enjoying, and loving others. You are fulfilling your soul's destiny. You took the bracelet Ruby gave you and unlocked the door to your soul. Many women are called, but few answer the call. You have realized that it is the journey, not the destination. I am most proud of you. The Goddess of All wants you to remember that you came to Earth to learn. Be in the moment. Smell the flowers." She winked. "In your culture, people smell the Starbucks."

Sophia nodded, enjoying the woman's sense of humor. "I think I understand."

The woman grasped her hands. "Let me show you my world, Sophia. A world of no prejudice, no hatred, no discrimination, and no wars. This is your heavenly home."

They floated above the cool green grass as if they were on a magic carpet. Sophia saw children laughing and playing. Young women gathered plants, read books, painted pictures, and played musical instruments. The sun sparkled off the shimmering waters of the flowing rivers and the fragrance of bountiful flowers filled her senses. A light breeze caressed her skin. She glanced down at her body and saw that she was dressed in an ethereal white gown. On her feet were tiny silver sandals.

They stopped in front of the large wooden doors of a mansion. The woman turned to her. "When it is your time, you will enter, but it is not time yet, or I'd ask you in for tea. You still have much work to do on Earth. You have art to produce, women to mentor, and your children to inspire. There will be grandbabies for you to love and cherish, and a special man will enter your life. You are the one destined to bring the divine divas to consciousness. You are the chosen one."

Why me? Why not my aunt, or a nun? What about those women who traveled to remote parts of the world and brought medicine and food? But as she stared into the woman's eyes, she realized the truth. "What am I the messenger of? How can I be of service?"

The woman smiled. "When the time is ripe, you will be told. You still need to have your croning ceremony." Her tone grew serious. "You will need to function as the wise woman for the girl Ben marries. She's going to need your wisdom. Your daughter will come around. You will have to let your mother go gracefully. Listen carefully to your heart and do what's right for you. It is your time now."

Sophia wondered who Ben was going to marry. How would Katie act in several years? What did she mean by let her mother go gracefully? She stared at the woman and nodded.

"It will all make sense when the time is ripe, my dear." The woman leaned over and gently kissed her on the forehead. "I am sending you back marked with the kiss of wisdom. Stay resourceful, be flexible, connected, and true to yourself. Just go down the road a piece and turn left at the large boulder."

Sophia found herself standing on the trail. The javelina was no where to be seen. Had that all been real? Or had she been hallucinating? She walked down the trail, turned left at the boulder, and headed to her car.

It was a warm afternoon, and Sophia found her aunt sitting in the garden reading. "I'm back."

Cassandra glanced up from her book, took off her glasses, and grinned. "Did you meet her?"

She slid into the lawn chair. "You mean the woman in the purple dress."

"Yes. Sophia. The goddess you were named after."

"I can't believe my mother named me after a goddess."

"Actually, it was our father's mother's name. She died before you were born. Our father always said she was as beautiful as a goddess."

She leaned against the back of the chair, her mind still swirling. "I'm confused. Why is she my name-sake? What do I do now?"

Cassandra smiled knowingly. "Why don't you think about it? The answer will come in the stillness of your mind. I'm going to get us some iced tea. I'm sure you're thirsty after your hike. After your hike tomorrow, you're going to visit Ruby. I'm certain she'll give you her blessing. Then we'll plan your croning ceremony to celebrate your fiftieth birthday."

"I have another hike? I thought you said I was done."

"You'll like this one. I promise." She stood and walked into the house.

Sophia watched her aunt walk away and sighed. No matter how hard she tried, she was still struggling with that word. Fifty. She was now eligible for the AARP card and as much as she had heard of the advantages of belonging to that club, it made her feel old. It was probably tucked into her mailbox in Reno. Soon they would mail her the early bird discounts for movies and restaurants. Of course she should think about her long term care.

Cassandra returned with a tall sweating glass. "Here, drink this. Rest. We'll skip yoga this afternoon. I think you've had enough for one day."

"Thanks." Sophia sipped the tea and closed her eyes. The warmth of the sun and the caress of the breeze against her bare skin lulled her to sleep, where she was transported to a lush green meadow brimming with colorful wildflowers. The heady smell intoxicated her as she felt her body sink into the ground and surrender to the aroma. She floated in the warm space.

"Sophia, Sophia. Open your eyes."

Sophia blinked and sat up. A kindly, elderly woman wearing a full white gown stood before her. Her gray hair was tightly curled, her eyes shadowed with blue, and her cheeks dotted with red rouge. "Who are you? Where am I?" Had she stepped into a storybook?

"Questions, questions. Fiddle-dee-dee. Fiddle-dee-dee." The elderly woman offered her tiny hand. "I am your Fairy Goodmother."

"My Fairy Godmother? What fairy tale am I in now?"

When the elderly woman smiled, tiny wrinkles jetted out from her gray eyes. "No, my dear. I am your Fairy Goodmother. I only dispense goodness." She touched Sophia's shoulder with her star-tipped wand, then waved it over her head. "Because you have hiked the trails and worked so hard at cleaning up your energy, I will grant you three wishes. These wishes must be based in loving kindness. Come, let's walk while you think about them."

Sophia struggled to her feet and took the woman's petite hand. They traveled as if on a magic carpet over the meadow. When animals approached, the fairy leaned over, caressed them, and whispered in their ears. When she touched them with her wand, they scampered off. The elderly woman's aura became lighter and lighter with each animal she met. "When one makes a wish based in goodness and truth, the universe has no reason not to grant it. Have you thought about your wishes, my dear?"

Sophia scratched her head, as she often did when facing a dilemma. If this was an ordinary fairy-tale adventure, she could ask for a million dollars, a new house, and a fabulous wardrobe. As she observed the Fairy Goodmother, she realized those wishes wouldn't work. "I don't know."

"Hold my hand tightly. We're going on a little trip," Fairy Goodmother said.

Sophia squeezed the woman's tiny hand. They lifted off the ground and soared through the sky. She glanced down at the planet and saw all the injustices imparted on people, mostly women. As they hovered over Africa, she shuddered as she witnessed what horrific things people did to young girls. Next the Fairy Goodmother transported her over the Middle East where she saw women wrapped in dark clothes, hiding their faces and bodies from the world. They flew over China where she saw women performing hard physical labor in the fields. They flew over other countries and saw women denied the freedoms Sophia had always taken for granted. She cried for the women whose children had been taken away from them, for the women who never had the opportunity to pursue their own dreams and desires, and for the millions of women around the world who struggled daily just to feed their families. As they soared over the United States, she felt the hunger in women's souls.

When they landed back in the meadow, the Fairy Goodmother smiled and waved her wand. "Are you ready, my dear?"

Sophia nodded and humbly asked for three wishes based in loving kindness. The Fairy Goodmother smiled, showing her approval. "I will grant the wishes because they are in loving kindness." Her blue eyes twinkled as she touched Sophia with her star-tipped wand. Sophia felt a surge of energy and heard a pop. She opened her eyes and discovered she was sitting in Cassandra's backyard, the ice in her tea had melted.

Chapter 16

Sophia parked in the lot and grabbed her backpack, excited and relieved because this was her last hike, unless Cassandra sprung something else on her. She glanced at the directions: *Follow the trail as it hugs the feet of the cliffs. The trail is rocky, so watch your footing.* She shook her head, a bit annoyed and said out loud, "Why can't this be easy?

She headed up the trail, carefully stepping on the red rocks. The last thing she needed was a twisted ankle. Who would she meet today? She breathed deeply, inhaling the clean air. There were times she felt this was all a dream, and that the divas were figments of her imagination. But whatever the divas were, they had helped her get to this place. She had healed her past, released the baggage she had carried around for years, and transformed her physical body. It was the future she was worried about. What was she going to do when she went back? She didn't have a job or a place to live. She wasn't going to fit in with her friends anymore. What would she say to them? If she tried to explain to the journey and how she'd met all these divas who told her incredible things and helped her find her way, they'd laugh and say she was becoming senile.

After she turned the corner and spotted a coyote standing in the middle of the trail, she came to a dead stop. She took a nervous, deep breath to gain enough courage to take a step forward and was surprised when the animal did not move. Did coyotes bite? Suddenly, the coyote transformed into a tall, lovely woman dressed in a short tunic and armed with a silver bow and quiver of arrows on her back. "I've been waiting for you, Sophia."

"Who are you?" Sophia reached back into her mind to find the mythology class she had taken in college. This woman looked familiar.

"I am Artemis. I live in the woods with the animals." All of a sudden, the trail filled with animals. The woman leaned over and petted several. "I am here to celebrate your new physical strength, your wildness, encourage you to develop new friendships, and celebrate the divine diva in you."

Sophia nodded. "I've been thinking about my friends on this trail. I don't think I'm going to fit in with any of them when I return."

The woman smiled lovingly. "That is because they will not understand where you're headed. I appear today to remind you of your independent feminine spirit that allows you to live like a diva."

Sophia stared at the tall woman. "What happened to the women of my generation? We used to have such passion."

The woman held out her hand, and she grasped it tightly. "Women have lost touch with their center. They are concerned with the physical and material world. They have lost their sense of humor. They refuse to reconcile the desire of an aging body, and they have refused to follow the journey. That is where you come in, Sophia."

"What do you mean by that?"

"All will be revealed in good time. Have patience. I am here to remind you that the later years can be the best years of your life. The events that you have endured—the collapse of your marriage and your children leaving the nest will free you to become your true self. That is, if you allow it. I am here to remind you to think young, explore new places, travel, strike out on new terrain, volunteer, and make a difference."

"I have no assignment this time."

The woman smiled. "Make this transition in your mind that you are an independent feminine spirit and a divine diva. You will receive instructions shortly." She leaned over and petted several rabbits, then told them, "I think you should all scamper now. There are hikers coming up the trail." The animals scurried away as instructed. The woman gave Sophia a slight brush of a kiss. "I will be watching over you. When you need some strength, think of me. Follow the trail a piece, and turn left at the large boulder."

That night Sophia dreamt she was walking along a sandy beach. The moon illuminated a path across the water. The beach was deserted. Water lapping gently against the shore was the only sound that broke the silence. She leaned over and picked up a piece of weathered driftwood and thought about the possibilities. She saw an elderly woman sitting on the beach crocheting a blanket.

"I've been expecting you, Sophia," the woman said.

She walked over to the woman. "Who are you?" At this point in her journey, she was no longer surprised by her encounters.

Putting down her golden crochet hook, the woman said, "I am Grandmother Spider Woman. I am the grandmother of the sun, the wind, and the corn. I am also the power of creativity. I am sent to help you weave the story you were destined to write that will help all women."

She sat next to the woman. "I can't write something for women. I paint, and I'm dabbling with a children's story. It has lots of pictures."

The woman gazed at her with her small dark eyes. "You are the messenger, Sophia. It is time the world receives this message. The fate of all women hangs on your shoulders. Take the knowledge you have learned, apply the skills you have kept dormant for years, and point women in the direction of their divine destiny. It has been said that the one who writes the story will create a new pattern and a new way of thinking." She smiled. "It is time, Sophia. The stars are aligned. You are the chosen one."

"Why me? I'm not worthy. Why not a woman who's been living this way for years? Cassandra? Mother Teresa? Doctor Myers? The woman in the art gallery? There must be hundreds of others who are more capable than me. I am not worthy of such a project."

The woman picked up her crochet hook and as she rapidly hooked the yarn, she hummed a song, a song Sophia remembered from childhood, a song her own grandmother used to sing to her. The melody unlocked passages deep in her mind as she traveled through time. She was a child sitting on the bedroom floor playing with her dolls. She watched as her younger self lined up the dolls and wove elaborate stories explaining the injustices of the world. She saw herself telling her sister the same tales when their parents had left them alone at night while they traveled the cocktail and country club scene. Then she saw herself as a young mother, captivating wide-eyed Ben and Katie with creative fables. She saw the children in the library gathering around her while she wove exotic mythological tales set in faraway places. "People seem to relate to myths and you've always been blessed with telling fairy tales," the woman said. She kept her eyes focused on her task. "That is why the journey seems like a fairy tale. Its roots are in childhood, which is sacred and divine. Remember, I will be right by your side to guide you as you weave the words. Use one of your paintings of the Red Rocks for the cover."

Sophia nodded. "I will do my best."

"Come, child. Give an old woman a kiss."

The following morning, while Sophia and Cassandra sat at the breakfast table, enjoying the sun streaming in through the windows, Sophia explained her dream to Cassandra. "I'm supposed to write this story. "I'm confused, but I didn't want to tell Grandmother Spider Woman that. She seemed so sure I am the one."

Cassandra reached for the bowl of strawberries and heaped several on her oatmeal. "It's good you're seeing Ruby today."

Sophia glanced up from her plate. "I have some questions I want answered. I hope she can help me."

Sophia drove the familiar road to the cabin. It was warm. The top was down and let the breeze rustle her hair. Cassandra had backed out of going at the last minute. A gallery owner had a client who wanted to commission a portrait of herself and daughter standing in the Red Rocks. "An artist dreams of this," her aunt said as she raced for the door.

Sophia parked in front of the cabin. The Spaniel lay on the porch, his tail thumping as she leaned over and petted his fur. She knocked on the screen door.

"Come in. I'm in the kitchen."

She entered the living room and made her way to the small kitchen. "Hi, Ruby."

Ruby turned around, wiping her hands on her floral apron. Her broad flat face beamed as she hugged Sophia. "What a pleasant surprise. My guides tell me you're ready. I've made some special tea." She poured two frosty glasses. "Let's go outside and sit under the tree. I've been cooking all morning, and I would love to get out of the kitchen."

Sophia took the tall plastic tumbler. "Tea sounds refreshing." Before taking the first drink, she wondered what concoction Ruby had added to this tea.

"Follow me." Ruby led her out into the backyard and over to several lounge chairs set up under large shade trees. She eased her short squat body into the chair and stretched out her legs. "That feels good."

Sophia sat down and sipped her tea. "I've completed the trails."

Ruby nodded. "I know. You have completed this part of the journey and you're discovering your voice."

"Cassandra's having a croning party for me in a few days. She's all excited."

Ruby laughed. "Cassandra loves any excuse to throw a party, besides, you deserve a party." She leaned over and touched her shoulder. "I see your transformation. No longer do you avert your eyes to your past, or numb your mind to escape reality. You *are* a divine diva."

Sophia nodded. "I do feel different. It's as if the past has finally left me. For the first time, I'm excited about the future. I realize I needed to strengthen my belief in the spiritual. That's what this journey has taught me. I don't think I ever truly believed before, but now that I have experienced things so wonderful. "I believe ... no, I know. I *am* sacred. I *am* a diva."

"A diva honors the path of every soul and allows them to explore themselves without judgment," Ruby said. "A diva finds her authentic voice of her divine soul and helps other women find theirs. The sacred aspect of the goddess is within every woman. Once upon a time, many years ago, all spirits were exhaled by Isis, the Mother of All, and set forth to begin its journey to enlightenment. Over time, women have lost their way because they have not listened to their hearts. That is why this journey was created."

"So what happens now? I have a croning ceremony, then what?" Sophia knew this wasn't the end of the trail.

"The croning ceremony is your initiation into the sisterhood of the wise women. Now you need to help others. You have been chosen to write a book to help other women reclaim their own divine diva."

"I still don't understand. Why me?"

"It is not for you to understand, Sophia. It is written in the stars. It is your destiny." Ruby smiled, sipping her tea.

Sophia sighed. The enormity of the task overwhelmed her. Term papers in college had beleaguered her, and she had often procrastinated over her school assignments. But write a book? "I don't even know where to start."

"Start at the dark night of your soul, which was necessary to start your journey," Ruby said. "Start when your nest emptied and your marriage and job failed. Weave the story so that women can see themselves and relate to your experience, Sophia. Reclaiming the divine diva is not forced. Many women refuse the call. They want to stay in the land of disillusion. They don't care if they spend their last penny on liposuction, Botox, or cosmetic surgery. They refuse to accept what is. But there are many women who know there's something more. They need your story. When a woman reclaims her divine diva, she will no longer fear death, separation, or aloneness. She will emerge transformed as she continues to walk through her physical life as a juicy, fully awakened woman. When she adopts the spiritual discipline of the Goddess, she nurtures the faiths of others. Christian, Judaism, Hinduism, Buddhism, Islam. It doesn't matter. They are all ways to the Divine."

"This is going to take me a while" Sophia said. "I haven't written anything since college. And that's been a few years."

"Everything you need is already inside of you. The divas wouldn't have picked you if they thought you weren't capable."

"Is there anything else I need to know?"

Ruby smiled. "You are on the right path, Sophia. A diva has wisdom, humor, compassion, courage, and energy. She knows herself. She accepts her flaws and imperfections. These qualities do not arrive overnight. They are acquired daily. Take what you have learned and help others and take care of yourself. You have spent your life caring for others. Now it is your time. I will see you at your croning. Goddess Bless."

* * *

"So, did Ruby clarify what you need to know?" Cassandra asked. "Did she give you her blessing?"

"Yes," Sophia said, "but I'm still supposed to write that book. Who's going to read it? It's going to detract from my painting, and I was on a roll."

"Perhaps your painting will flow because of the story," Cassandra said. "I have great success when I mix art mediums." She beamed. "Now we need to plan your party."

She studied her aunt. "Don't go all out for this. Can't we just invite a few people? I've never been one for the spotlight."

"Nonsense. You have earned this. Think of all the women who've never made it to fifty and had a party to celebrate their croning. They died in childbirth, were ravaged by cancer or disease, or taken prematurely in an accident. Turning fifty is a celebration. It's time for a party!"

Sophia chuckled. "I remember when Brad turned fifty. He sulked for a week. When his AARP card turned up in the mailbox, he threw a tantrum and ripped it up." She laughed. "Then he had to have a colonoscopy." Did that mean she would have to have one? She'd think about it later.

"Men are usually a little childish about things like that," Cassandra said.

"That's true, and now he's going to marry a child. How fitting."

"I don't want to be nosey, but how is the divorce going? You got some papers in the mail the other day."

"My lawyer's been great. She's handled everything. Brad wants this over with in a hurry so he can marry Leslie. Katie's dropped several hints about Leslie being pregnant. Probably so I won't go crazy when I find out. It's pathetic. Brad's fifty-two. He wasn't around much when Ben and Katie were little, but now he's going to have another child and be the perfect father."

"Maybe Leslie isn't as stupid as you think she is," Cassandra pointed out. "Having a child will keep her hands in Brad's income for years to come."

"Hmmm, I hadn't thought about that. If that's the case, then it serves him right. He'll be working well into his seventies." She laughed. "Maybe they'll have twins. Double the expenses. When we were first married, he said he wanted to retire by the time he was fifty-five." She paused. "I'm going to call my friend Brenda. She'll know what's going on. I'm curious."

"We were just talking about you the other day at lunch," Brenda said. "No one's seen or heard from you. I'm worried. I ran into Brad with this young woman at the club. The rumor is that you two are divorcing."

"That woman he's with must be Leslie. My replacement."

There was silence on the other end of the phone. "I'm so sorry, Sophia. What happened?"

"He fell in love with her. I found out, confronted him, and he didn't deny it. I left and went to visit my aunt."

"The artist?"

"Yes." She started to explain her adventures, but then decided against it. Brenda wouldn't understand. She was one of those women who was only concerned with her physical appearance, spending hundreds of dollars each year on cosmetic procedures and potions promising to the erase the years. Several times a year she traveled to San Francisco where she ran up outrageous amounts on her husband's credit card. "I've gotten back into painting. I even have several at a gallery."

"The gossip around the club is that Leslie's pregnant, and as soon as your divorce is final he's going to marry her. It looks like she has a little bit of a tummy. Something's gotten into Brad. He's acting like an adolescent. He's even wearing a gold chain and bracelet."

Sophia stretched her legs. "He's with a child who obviously doesn't want him to look like the old man that he is. But I wish them well. I need to go forward."

"That doesn't sound like the same Sophia I know. What happened to you?"

"Nothing. I've been painting. I hike everyday, and I go to yoga. That's about it. It's pretty quiet here"

"Sophia," Brenda said. "I have another call. It was good talking to you. We're all here for you when you return."

Sophia set the phone down. Brenda and her gang would disown her as soon as the ink was dry on her divorce papers. She remembered watching the group reject Debbie Barnes last year when her husband left her for his therapist, but Sophia realized she didn't care anymore. Artemis had been right. She had nothing in common with those women any more. The only reason Sophia had called Brenda was to find out the dirt on Brad and Leslie. And as usual, Brenda had delivered. She imagined Brenda was calling all her friends with the news.

Sophia went looking for Cassandra and found her in her studio. "I was right. Leslie's pregnant."

Her aunt roared with laughter. "Serves the jerk right. He'll be sitting through those long Little League games in his golden years. Men." She shook her head as if to indicate that she would never understand them. "By the way, your croning is in five days. Don't you have to write something first?"

Sophia sunk into a chair. "But where do I start? How can I write a book in five days?"

"Crones don't whine," Cassandra reminded her. "You start by going into my study, turning on the computer, and writing."

"But."

"No buts. It is your destiny. Now scoot. You have five days."

"But I have an appointment with Kurt." She didn't want to miss his hands traveling her body.

"I suggest you put it off until you're done with the story," Cassandra said. She winked. "He'll wait."

Sophia locked herself into the tiny, cluttered office. She was surprised as the story flowed and her fingers hammered away at the keyboard. A flood tide of raw creative energy consumed her. She came out only for meals, shunning yoga and hiking, refusing phone calls, and sending Cassandra and Dave to the Internet for research materials. Her aunt was right—the story materialized in her mind as her fingers danced across the keys.

On the day of her croning, she typed the words. *The End.* She turned off the computer, gathered the papers, and emerged from the office. "I'm finished!"

Cassandra came running. "Congratulations. You did it. Why don't you take a shower, and I'll make you a special breakfast. The women are arriving at noon."

"Can I just take a nap?" Sophia asked. "I didn't sleep last night. I wanted to get it finished."

Her aunt leaned over and kissed her lightly on the cheek. "I'll wake you up at eleven-thirty."

She slipped under the cool sheets and quickly fell asleep. For once there were no rendezvous with exotic goddesses, no travels to foreign worlds, and no messages or instructions. Just pure blissful sleep.

Chapter 17

The women stood in a circle in Cassandra's backyard. The sky was cloudless and a light breeze ruffled the trees. Cassandra wore a flowing purple gown and stood in the middle of the circle. Many of the other women wore purple, some wore red. Sophia wore a purple tunic and jeans. Cassandra raised her arms to the sky. "We are gathered here on this glorious May day to celebrate my niece's croning. This ancient rite of passage has been created to honor women as they enter their wisdom years. Sophia is coming of age, accessing her wisdom, and reclaiming the divine diva."

The women clapped and cheered. A woman with short red hair standing next to Sophia leaned over and whispered, "Don't believe a thing the media reports about aging, honey. The best is yet to be."

Sophia smiled at the woman, whom she judged to be somewhere in her sixties, and glanced around the group of women. Ruby caught her eye and smiled, her long gray hair plated in braids. She wore an Indian dress accented with purple beading.

Cassandra continued her speech. "Society tells us that aging is wicked, especially if you're a woman. We all know that is a lie because we are all testimonials to the fact that the older woman is full of beauty, wisdom, and energy. I want to thank each of you for attending this ceremony as we guide Sophia into her wisdom years. The word crone is a recent women's reclamation. Literature and history have portrayed the crone as a shriveled, cold, and bitter old woman, but that was not always true. Originally, many thousands of years ago, the crone was the wise woman, the keeper of the blood. She functioned as a teacher for those younger. She followed her inner guidance and knew the truth about the cycle of life because of the acquired knowledge during her long journey. Usually women at this stage of life have experienced and accepted loneliness, divorce, illness, the empty nest and have spent many hours pondering life's meaning.

"Today we gather to help Sophia accept this, to reclaim her divine diva instead of mourn what she once was and had." Cassandra smiled at Sophia. "I'd like us all to gather hands. Ruby is going to lead us in prayer." Cassandra walked back to the circle and took Sophia's hand.

Ruby walked into the middle carrying her drum. The women gathered hands. Ruby began beating the drum, singing a song about the blessings of an abundant life, and the sacredness of becoming the wise woman. She reverted to her native tongue. The words were strange, yet comforting. The women swayed to the beat. Finally, Ruby stopped and walked over to Sophia and handed her the drum. "This is my gift to you. Make beautiful music with it—sing your story. This drum was made many years ago by a wise woman from my tribe. I give you my blessings."

Sophia held the exquisite drum in her hands. "Thank you, Ruby. I am honored." Ruby smiled proudly and went back to her place.

Cassandra walked to the middle of the circle and lit the logs in the small fire pit. The logs caught fire and burned. She sprinkled herbs over the burning logs, then turned to the women. "We will share with Sophia the wisdom we have learned since our own croning. Who wants to start?"

Martha, a tall woman dressed in a purple gown and wearing large purple sunglasses raised her hand. "I'll start." She smiled at Sophia. "I'm Martha and I recently turned sixty-five. I stand here today to welcome your into the third phase of life. I'll be honest. I used to fear it, but once I stepped over the threshold and shed my former way of thinking, I discovered that the fear was unfounded. I was so moved when I recognized that I was going to die and that living is dying and dying is a part of living. Something in me awakened. I realized that life was not a dress rehearsal. It was my time to do what I wanted to do. I raised four children, nurtured a husband, helped his career, took care of his parents in their old age, and volunteered everywhere. I decided to do what I wanted to do and not what other people wanted me to do. So you know what I did?"

"No, what?" Sophia was intrigued by this interesting woman. Martha stood tall and stately, adjusting her glasses on her patrician nose.

"I went back to college. In my day, when a woman graduated from college and married, as soon as she had a child, she was expected to stay home and tend the children and house. I was on the fringe of the women's movement. I lived in a small town in the Mid-West. My first degree was in elementary education, which was so typical of my generation. I never even taught. My first child was born nine months after I was married, thanks to the rhythm method taught by the Catholic Church," she said sarcastically. "When I first went back to school, I got my Masters in Education. Now I'm working on my Ph.D. I hope to teach at the college level. My husband and children have been supportive, especially my grandchildren. They like the fact that Grandma goes to school. It's been wonderful."

Sophia smiled with admiration at Martha, thinking that going back to school and taking art classes could be an option for her as well.

"Thank you, Martha. Let's continue. Who's next?" Cassandra asked.

The athletic-looking woman next to Martha raised her hand. "I'm Denise." She paused, then laughed. "For a moment I forgot how old I am. I'm sixty-eight. I was croned about ten years ago. When I turned fifty, there wasn't this kind of support system around. I think it's wonderful. It's a celebration of our mature age. Since the patriarchy doesn't

183

seem to value older women, we celebrate and value ourselves. It's marvelous. I've done things now that I would have never done when I was younger." Denise laughed. "I used to fear everything, but now that I'm older and I understand the finality of my existence, I'm willing to take more risks. I've endured my share of losses, but that has helped me accept the fragility of life and its wonderful treasures. Eight years ago, I lost my husband of forty years, and instead of sitting home and crying like an old woman, I jumped into life. I've climbed Macchu Picchu, hiked into the Amazon jungle, gone white water rafting, jumped out of a plane, and backpacked through the Rockies." She grinned. "Someone once said that my husband would have loved taking those adventures with me, but I disagreed. Dave would have hated them. He would have been upset that there was no toilet, the room was too narrow, and the bed, if there was a bed, was too short. No, Dave was not one for adventure, unless it was on a big screen. We had forty good years, three wonderful children, but now it's my time and I'm enjoying every minute."

Sophia studied Denise intently, thinking that Dave sounded a bit like Brad. She had wanted adventures, but the only adventures he would consider were the ones that involved five-star hotels with multiple amenities. But it didn't matter anymore. He could have those adventures with Leslie and the baby. She smiled wickedly.

Another woman took the circle "I'm Sandra. I'm fifty-five. I was croned several years ago in this very backyard." She let out a smile of gratitude toward Cassandra. "It was the best thing that ever happened to me. I've watched so many of my friends fight the aging process. I wanted to be different. To accept what is. So I changed careers. After my son left for college, I went back to school and became a floral designer. I love working with flowers. It brings me great joy. My husband and I have had our difficulties, but we're still together. My son is getting married this July. My life is blessed. Congratulations, Sophia. Welcome to this wonderful world of juicy crones."

Sophia listened as the women continued with their stories. They went around the circle, and by the time they got to the last woman, Sophia felt energized.

"It's your turn to tell the group what you've learned," Cassandra whispered.

Sophia stepped out into the circle of women and, as nervous as she was, she managed a smile, as they had all done before speaking. "Thank you for your wonderful stories. I have never felt so loved and accepted as I do right now. I have to be honest. Before I came to stay with Cassandra, I was terrified. My husband had left me for a younger woman. I was fired from my job that I was really not that good at, and my kids were away at college and didn't need me any longer. But that's all changed. I've come to terms with my husband's betrayal. I've had a great deal of time to reflect about my marriage, and in retrospect, I understand now that we didn't have much of a marriage. I married him on the rebound. I loved being a mother, but we all know that job isn't forever. My husband and I had nothing in common but the children, and when the children left?" She shrugged. "It's the same tired plot as many daytime soaps."

Sophia glanced around the circle. The woman smiled and nodded in agreement. They understood her story. She continued. "When I came here and chose to claim my divine diva, I had to come to terms with my problem of anorexia and my anger at the Catholic Church. Cassandra helped me do that. You wouldn't have recognized me when I arrived. I'm fifteen pounds heavier now and I feel terrific. I'm stronger than I have ever been and I have so much energy. I was also angry—angry at God. But on this journey, I discovered the female aspect of God, which resonates with me and I've found her everywhere. She has helped me release my creativity and accept myself. For the first time in my life, I feel empowered.

I know what I want to be when I grow up. I see so many women fighting the aging process. The women I used to hang around with spent their days rushing around town to get their hair colored, their bodies nipped and tucked, and their faces pulled so they could mold into society's norms. They spent money they didn't have on products that promised to erase years, and I was following in their footsteps. Now I've changed. I don't want to erase my years. I'm proud of who I am and what I have done with my life so far. I am ready to claim the crone in me."

The women cheered. Cassandra walked into the circle and hugged her. "Now it's time for refreshments. Come, ladies, let's eat." Cassandra led the women to the patio that was adorned with an array of food and drinks. She unwrapped platters of cold meats, cheeses, fruit, and vegetables. While the women formed a line, Cassandra hurried into the kitchen and returned with several baskets filled with rolls. "You start first, Sophia. There's cake when we're all done."

Sophia started the line, took a warm roll, cut it in half, and layered it with meat and cheese slices. She spread a thin layer of mayonnaise, something she would have never done in her former life, and took several baby carrots. She even placed a large dollop of dip on her plate. She sat down and was joined shortly by several women. Leila sat next to her. "I have terrific news, Sophia. We sold one of your paintings yesterday. A woman from New York bought it. She asked about the artist, so I told her all about you."

"Someone actually bought one of my paintings?" Sophia asked.

"I told you they would. You're good. You just have to believe in yourself. Cassandra says you've been hard at work on another project. Is it something I can hang in the gallery?"

"I don't think so," Sophia said. "Maybe someday." *Okay, here goes. Tell the world.* "It's a book."

"You wrote a book," a woman with short red hair exclaimed. She sat down by Sophia. "How fabulous! When did you start writing?"

Sophia blushed. "Just recently. I had some help."

"Who helped you?" Leila asked.

"It was the divas."

Leila's eyes widened. "Then you're the chosen one." She hugged Sophia. "You need an editor."

"Probably. I wrote it in five days and writing isn't my thing."

Leila stood up and scanned the yard. "There's Fran. She used to be an editor at one of the big publishing houses back east. She can help." Leila excused herself and walked over and whispered to the woman. The woman turned around and stared at Sophia. Leila led the woman over. "Sophia's done it," Leila explained.

"What have you done, dear?" Fran asked, sitting next to her. Fran appeared to be in her early seventies. Her silver hair was styled in a pageboy cut, and she wore enormous tortoise shell glasses and heavy eye makeup. Her voice was hoarse and scratchy, as if she had smoked for years.

Sophia swallowed nervously, as if to delay answering. "I wrote the story about the journey."

"The journey we've all taken?" Fran asked.

She nodded.

"When can I see it?"

"You can have it, but I'm going to warn you. It's really rough." Sophia had worked so hard on it that she never wanted to see it again. She wanted to paint, not write. And her wrist hurt from that stupid keyboard.

"I'll edit it. I was quite good in my day. You did save it to disk?" Fran asked.

"It's on Cassandra's hard drive."

"This is a day for celebration," Fran exclaimed. "The world will realize the power of the Goddess. Women everywhere will want to claim their own divine diva." She stood. "Ladies, I have an announcement. The book has been written." The women crowded around her, cheering and yelling. "This calls for champagne," Fran exclaimed. "Cassandra, pop the cork."

* * *

In her dreams that night, Sophia walked along a path by a desert lake. It was twilight—the shadows lengthened in the diminishing sunlight. She followed the path through the sagebrush, and as the sun faded behind the horizon line, the full moon bathed the trail for her. She wrinkled her nose as the familiar smell of lilacs and lavender aroused her senses. Ahead on the trail sat a golden chariot; its passenger was the beautiful woman dressed in a flowing white gown. "It's time you knew my name, Sophia," the woman said. "I am Isis. The Goddess of All. Come, let me take you for a ride."

Sophia bowed for she was in the presence of the most holy. She climbed into the chariot. Isis waved her golden wand, and they flew across the desert and up into the night sky. Sophia glanced down and saw the millions of women struggling with their mortality and aging. She saw husbands leaving their wives for younger women, women crying late into the night because they were old and alone and their children too busy to visit. She saw women displaced by the job market and struggling to make ends meet, and she realized the thirst in women's souls. They had lost their soul connection. She understood that the book she had written would help those who read and incorporated its teachings to find their own truth. Isis took Sophia's hand into her own.

"I have appeared because you have retrieved the lost pieces of your soul. You have completed the journey and claimed your divine diva. I thank you for writing the book. My hope is that it will change the way society views older women. You have opened the door for all women." Isis squeezed her hand. "You don't need to be helped any longer. You know what to do from now on."

Sophia nodded, feeling soothed and protected in this beautiful woman's presence. She wished Isis would stay with her always because she felt safe and secure, but she realized this was a fleeting moment. "I am ready to serve."

Isis smiled. "I know, my dear. This is what I want you to do." She whispered into her ear, kissed her gently on the cheek, and waved her wand.

Sophia awoke in the bedroom and glanced around. The house was silent. No goddesses stood in her room. Outside it was dark. She stretched her legs, fixed her eyes at the ceiling, and realized the enormity of her future and the task that lay ahead.

Chapter 18

Sophia opened the door. Kurt stood with his back to her arranging a towel on the massage table. Her knees wobbled. God, he was gorgeous. Why was he interested in her? "Hi, Kurt."

He turned around, his sandy blond hair brushing his blue eyes, and grinned. "It's nice to see you, Sophia. I've been waiting for you." She set her purse down. She had never had a massage by a man before and felt uncomfortable exposing her fifty-year-old body to this hunk. "Why don't you slip out of your clothes and slide under the towel, face down." He winked. "I'll be good. I promise." He walked out of the room. "I'll be back in a few minutes."

Sophia slid out of her clothes and slipped under the towel, trying to remember the last time she had had a massage. It had to be at least ten years ago. She and Brad had gone to a resort for their anniversary and while he was on the golf course, she treated herself to a massage and facial in the spa. But that had been years ago, when her skin was tighter.

There was a knock and he entered. He dimmed the lights, lit several candles, and turned on the stereo. "Do you have any aches I should concentrate on?" he asked, while opening a bottle of oil and pouring some into his hands. "I'm going to be using essential oils on you. I want you to close your eyes and enjoy."

Sophia thought about the ache in her heart, but that wasn't the type of ache he was talking about. "No. My calves are a little sore from all that hiking Cassandra's made me do." She felt his hands on her back, his fingers massaging her muscles, the smell of the lavender oil filling the room. His hands felt like magic as they worked the kinks out of her back. "That feels wonderful. I've forgotten how good this feels."

"Just relax, Sophia. Let your mind drift."

She felt herself slip away as he worked her body. After he had finished with her back, his hands traveled to her legs, where he applied deep pressure to her calves. When he reached her feet, she squealed.

"You're sensitive there," he joked, as his hands gripped her feet. He asked her to turn over, and he began working again. She knew she was supposed to keep her eyes closed, but she squinted. "Close your eyes, Sophia. No peeking."

Sophia closed her eyes, but her mind was in overdrive. Part of her really wanted to sleep with him. The old Sophia would have never felt like this, or if she had, she would have been too guilt-ridden to do anything about it, but the new Sophia was eager. Was this her diva power? Was this the zest of being a crone Cassandra talked about? Was she going to become some middle-aged sex machine? She hadn't had thoughts like this since she was a teenager. Her mind continued its tirade.

"Relax, Sophia," he said as he lifted her arms. "You're not letting go."

No, I only want to let go into your arms. How can I meditate with you massaging my body? I'm not a nun. I'm just some middle-aged woman who hasn't had sex in months. She closed her eyes and focused on her breathing. *Thank God for yoga.* At least she had learned something.

He started at the top of her head. She felt his hands work her face, her head. *Ah, this is heaven.* Then he stroked her ears. She never knew someone touching her ears could feel so good. He leaned over and kissed her forehead. She opened her eyes quickly.

"I'm sorry," he said. "I usually don't do that, but I couldn't resist. How do you feel?"

Sophia blinked. "Fantastic. Thank you." *But I really want to pull you down, rip off all your clothes, and seduce you.*

"I think that's probably enough for today. I'll be outside when you're ready." Kurt washed his hands and left the room.

She lay on the table, staring at the ceiling. Had she made a fool of herself? What was she thinking? He probably thought she was some batty old woman. She got off the table, dressed, and looked at her reflection in the mirror. Her hair stood out in all directions. She reached into her purse, found her brush, and tried to make sense out of her hair.

She opened the door to Kurt's office and found him sitting at his desk writing. "Are you sure I can't pay you anything?"

He glanced up. "No. It was on the house. But you can do one thing for me."

Anything, she thought. *Name it.* "Sure."

"Join me for dinner tonight. My house. I'm quite a good cook, if I do say so myself."

"I'd like that. Thank you."

"Let me jot down the directions," he said. He scribbled a map on a piece of paper. "You shouldn't have too much trouble finding it. Seven, okay?"

"Seven is fine. Thank you."

Cassandra met her at the door. "How was it?"

"He invited me for dinner. What am I going to wear? Nothing fits anymore."

"Then I suggest we go shopping. I know the perfect place."

Several hours later they returned with their arms filled with bags. Cassandra had taken her to the Arts and Craft Village filled with shops, restaurants, and galleries. The plaza had the ambiance of an old Mexican village. Sophia had gone wild, running up her MasterCard with new purchases, choosing bohemian tops, flowing skirts, large earrings, and strappy sandals. She didn't know how she was going to pay for all of it, but she figured she'd deal with that later. Next week she planned to return to Reno to clean out the house and take the things she wanted before she and Brad met with the mediator to divide their assets.

Sophia took a shower, lathering her body with almond-scented wash, then toweled off, and slipped into her new skirt and top. After styling her hair and applying light makeup, she apprised herself in the mirror. *Not too bad*, she decided. *I look ten years younger than when I arrived in Sedona.* Her eyes twinkled, her face was clear and tanned, and her skin looked firmer. She looked closer. Even the fine lines around her mouth and eyes had diminished. Cassandra was right. The new pounds, the new muscles, and the fresh air had been all the anti-aging medicine she needed. Who needed Botox and collagen? After slicking her lips with gloss, she headed towards the car.

Kurt lived only several blocks from Cassandra. Sophia pulled into his driveway and turned off the engine. The house was a small bungalow surrounded by blooming flower beds and a rock garden. The sounds of Eric Clapton resonated from inside. She knocked on the door.

"Come on in. I'm in the kitchen," he yelled.

Sophia opened the door and entered a foyer filled with plants and a skylight beaming down on them. To the right, a cozy living room shone with polished hardwood floors and leather couches. The walls were painted red, which accented the Indian artwork scattered on the walls. It was hard to believe that a man lived here alone. Her heels clicked as she walked on the floor and entered the kitchen.

Kurt stood at the sink washing his hands. He turned around and whistled. "Don't you look good? You're just in time to help."

She blushed and set her purse down. "Of course. What can I do?"

He pointed to a bottle of Pinot Noir and two glasses. "Why don't you pour the wine? I'm almost done."

She inhaled. "What are you cooking because it smells wonderful?"

Kurt grinned. "I hope you like lamb."

"I haven't had it in years."

"I'm pretty proud of this dish. It's wine-braised leg of lamb with garlic, white beans, tomatoes, and spinach."

"Where did you learn to cook?" She handed him a glass of wine.

"After my divorce, I took several cooking classes. One of my friends said it was a great place to meet women."

She laughed. "You're probably right." She sipped the wine. "This is excellent."

"I've always been fond of Pinot Noir. This one comes from Santa Barbara County. Have you ever gone wine-tasting?"

Sophia sat at the pine kitchen table and nodded. "Reno isn't that far from the Napa Valley. At least once a year, my husband and I would take a trip, visit several of the wineries, and load up on wine. When we moved into our new house, he built this elaborate wine cellar. He's quite proud of it. I used to find him sitting in it, sipping wine and admiring his collection."

Kurt pointed to a wine rack and laughed. "That's my wine collection. Someday when I'm rich I'll have a wine cellar. I've always wanted to own a winery. I think I'd like working in the fields all day."

"Your garden is beautiful," Sophia said as she gazed out the kitchen window into the lush backyard. "You're good with your hands." She blushed. "I meant with plants."

He grinned, his eyes twinkling. "I like to work with my hands. Why don't we sit in the living room? Dinner will be ready in a half hour. Are you hungry?"

"Famished." She followed him into the living room and sunk into the leather couch. He sat next to her, his leg brushing hers, sending electric shocks up her legs. He asked her questions about her children. She described Ben and Katie and the feelings she had felt when they left home.

"I was the last child to leave home," he said. "My mother fell into a deep depression, but then my older sister had twins and that cured it." He laughed. "I have seven nieces and nephews and that keeps her busy."

"Did you ever want children?"

"At first I did, but my wife Karen was too busy with her career. Then we divorced and I developed other interests. I'll be forty soon. I think I'm past that time."

She laughed. "People have children in their forties and fifties all the time now." She grinned as she thought of her almost ex-husband.

"I'm too set in my ways," Kurt said. "I see my nieces and nephews and I'm the one they call when they have a problem. Several of them have stayed with me for a period of time. It's okay. I'm not missing anything."

She finished her wine. He reached for the bottle and refilled their glasses. "Are you trying to get me drunk?" she teased.

"No. Just loose and relaxed." He grinned and glanced at his watch. "The lamb is about done."

They dined in the candle-lit kitchen. He entertained her with stories of his childhood and college years. She edited her own stories as she told them. When they finished, he served coffee and cheese cake. As he set a dish down for her, the old Sophia started to push the dessert away. *Too many calories.* She saw her mother wag her finger, but the new Sophia triumphed. She picked up her spoon and took a bite. "This is delicious."

"I confess. I didn't make this."

"Then you're not so perfect after all?"

"No. I'm afraid not." He grinned.

They finished their dessert and stacked the dishes in the sink. "Don't you want to wash them?" she asked.

He reached for her hand. "No. I have other things I'd rather do. They'll be there in the morning." He led her into the bedroom. "If you're too uncomfortable, we can just cuddle. But correct me if I'm wrong. I think you feel the same way about me that I feel about you."

Sophia nodded, unsure of her emotions. She hadn't had sex with another man since she married Brad, and that was two children and twenty-three years ago. She was scared, but she didn't want him to know it.

He dimmed the lights. *Thank God,* she thought. *I look much better in softer light.*

Kurt lit several candles, and turned on a small CD player. The gentle sounds of classical music flowed as he gathered her into his arms. "You're a remarkable woman, Sophia. You make me want to be the best I am when I'm around you."

She watched him fumble with her buttons. "Here. Let me help you." She unbuttoned her blouse and took off her bra.

"You're beautiful," he said huskily as he slid out of his clothes.

And you're much younger than me. Is this why Brad chose Leslie? Was it the touch of young skin? But the divine diva in her rose up and chased the thoughts away. He led her to the bed, lifted her up, then gently set her down.

"I'm nervous."

"Don't be," he said softly. "I won't do anything you don't want me to."

Sophia awoke to the sunlight streaming through the windows and glanced to the other side of the bed. It was vacant. She stared at the ceiling and contemplated last night. It had been magical. Kurt had proved to be an amazing lover, gentle, courteous, and playful. So unlike Brad, whose idea of sex was the same position on the same night of the week, never giving any thought of her needs.

Kurt came into the room carrying a tray filled with coffee, fruit, and toast. "Good morning, sleepyhead. I was afraid you were going to sleep all day."

Sophia scooted up in bed. "What time is it?"

"Almost ten. I have an appointment soon." He sat next to her and handed her a cup of coffee. He kissed her cheek. "Thank you for last night."

She blushed. "No. I should be thanking you. You made me feel so loved and alive. I can't remember the last time I felt like that."

He smiled. "I feel the same way. I just want you to know that I'm not the kind of guy who goes to bed with every woman he meets. I know this will blow the gossip around town, but this is the first time for me since my divorce."

"Thank you for making me feel special. I'll get out of your hair so you can get to your appointment." She started to get up.

"When can I see you again?"

"I'm leaving in a week. I have to go home and clean up some loose ends."

"Dinner tonight?" he asked. "I'll take you out."

She smiled seductively. "No. I'll cook for you. I don't want to waste time sitting in restaurants dreaming about being in bed."

Sophia spent her final week in Sedona painting, hiking, and in Kurt's arms in the evenings. One night they joined Cassandra and Dave for dinner, but left soon after. Her aunt grinned as she walked them to the door. "He's magnificent, Sophia," she said in a low voice so Kurt would not hear. "He has wonderful energy. I'm so pleased for you."

Sophia blushed. "I wish I didn't have to go home, but the kids are coming home after classes end and of course I have to baby-sit Ben."

"Planes fly between Phoenix and Reno," her aunt reminded her. "After you get your life together, you might want to think about relocating here. It's a good place for you to paint. You can move in with me for awhile if you want."

"Thanks, Cassandra. I really appreciate that, but if I move here I will get my own place. Kurt's been pestering me to move to this area. It's just the kids." Sophia thought about the irony of the situation.

"Why don't you ask the Goddess?" her aunt suggested. "She always knows what to do."

That night Sophia prayed to the Goddess, then fell asleep. She dreamt she was walking through the woods. Isis appeared and touched her with her golden wand again. "I am happy for you, Sophia. You are in training to be a crone. You wrote the book. The universe will see that it is accepted, but it is not quite time for you to abandon your responsibilities. He will wait for you."

"But I've given my children my life. They don't need me anymore," she wailed.

"All in good time, my dear. All in good time." Isis waved her wand.

There was a knock at the door and Cassandra entered the room. She shook her gently "Sophia, it's Brad. He says it's urgent."

She struggled out of a deep sleep. "Tell him he can talk to my lawyer."

"It has nothing to do with your divorce. It's Katie. She's been in a horrible accident."

Chapter 19

Sophia threw her clothes into the suitcases and raced to the car. Cassandra stood outside, tears filling her eyes. "Are you sure you don't want me to come with you?"

"I need the windshield time. I have a lot to think about." Sophia studied her aunt. "Thank you so much for everything you've done for me. This has been an amazing journey. I couldn't have done it without you."

"You are a brilliant woman, Sophia. I am so proud of you. Please try and not worry about Katie. It is out of your hands. All you can do is pray."

She nodded sadly, as she threw her suitcases in the back seat, then turned to her aunt. "Oh, my God, Cassandra. What if she doesn't make it?"

Cassandra's tone grew grave. "You can't think that. She's going to be okay. She'll come out of that coma. Thankfully she was wearing her seat belt."

"At least she listened to me about that. I still can't believe that she took Brad's car to a party, drank too much liquor, and slammed into someone's stone fence. I'm a terrible mother. I should have been home."

Cassandra grabbed Sophia by the shoulders. "Just remember what you've learned on your journey and apply that wisdom. Remember that the real test of womanhood is when you stand alone on your foundation. The journey is never over." She kissed her lightly on the cheek. "I will be praying for you both."

Sophia slid into the car, started the engine, and pulled out onto the road. She thought that if she didn't stop she'd be home by tomorrow afternoon. She waved to her aunt and sped toward the highway. Her hands quivered as she gripped the steering wheel. Katie was in the hospital with two broken legs, several cracked ribs and a dislocated shoulder. The doctor had told Sophia over the phone that Katie was lucky because there wasn't any internal damage, but she was in a coma and they didn't know why. They assured Sophia that Katie would awaken soon and then she was going to need physical therapy and care for several months.

But what if she doesn't wake up? The doctors don't understand why she's in a coma, so why are they sure she'll wake up. One doctor suggested that she didn't want to wake up and face the consequences of her actions. Another one said it was her body's way of healing. Why didn't they know? Hadn't they gone to medical school for years? Didn't they play God daily and charge outrageous fees?

Okay, okay. She remembered her lessons. Show compassion, forgive, let go of the past. But goddesses or not, she was angry with Katie. *What had possessed her to go home for the weekend before finals, which of course she won't take now because she's in a coma and can't possibly finish the semester? Why would she drive Brad's beloved Porsche to that party by the university because some boy she had gone to high school with had called and convinced her to get there as quickly as she could?*

What had possessed Katie to drink and drive? Hadn't she drilled that into the kids enough when they were growing up? Didn't Katie remember Eric Brown, the young man from her class who had rammed his car into a tree one summer evening before the start of her senior year? In the wreckage, the cops had discovered an empty bottle of rum. She remembered the agony of his parents at the funeral. Eric had been an only child.

Sophia turned onto the highway and increased her speed. *It was my fault. If I hadn't come to Sedona this wouldn't have happened. I would have never allowed Katie to come home for a party so close to finals. If I would have been home, she wouldn't have had the opportunity to coerce Brad to let her drive his car. I would have reminded her to call if she needed a ride home.*

God, I feel so guilty. What kind of mother am I?

She stopped outside of Las Vegas for gas and a hamburger. She called the hospital again. The nurse said there was no change in Katie's condition. Her father and step-mother had just stepped out for something to eat. Sophia wanted to scream at the woman that Leslie wasn't the step-mother yet; the divorce was not final, but she remembered the words of the divas. *God, this spiritual stuff is hard work. Life was much easier as a spiritual dropout.*

Sophia continued driving and thought about Kurt. Already she missed his touch, the way he held her in his strong arms, and the way he listened when she talked. It was as if she had something important to say. He made her feel loved and special, something she hadn't felt in a very long time. *Shit. I shouldn't be thinking about him now when Katie was so sick. What's wrong with me? What kind of mother would be thinking about a man she barely knew when her daughter is lying in a hospital room in a coma?*

She realized she'd have to face Brad when she returned. They only spoke through their lawyers about the divorce, but this was different. Their child was in trouble.

"This is a test," a voice close by said.

Sophia glanced at the passenger seat and saw Isis, with her golden gown neatly tucked around. "You scared me," Sophia said.

Isis smiled. "Do not be afraid. I am always with you. Remember the lessons you've learned and the power you've released. Let go of the guilt. It is not your fault. All beings have free will."

She swerved to avoid a car that changed lanes abruptly. "I've got to pay attention, or I'm going to get us killed." She glanced at Isis. "Or me, anyways."

Isis touched her lightly on her shoulder. "Surround yourself with white light and you will be protected. Use the gifts you've uncovered and remember it is the journey, not the destination that matters." She leaned over and kissed Sophia lightly on the cheek.

Sophia started to ask if Katie was really going to be okay like the doctors had said, but Isis had vanished. Tears filled Sophia's eyes, but she surrounded herself with white light and focused on her drive home.

Hours later she pulled into the hospital parking lot and searched for a parking place, finally snagging one by the dumpster. Exhausted and noticing her own unpleasant odor because she had not taken the time to bathe before she left, she dragged her tired body out of the car. She entered the hospital and took the elevator to the fourth floor.

"Can I help you?" the nurse who stood behind the counter asked.

"I'm looking for Katie Roberts. I'm her mother."

"Follow me." The nurse led her down the sterile corridor and opened the door to a sunny room. In the middle of the room, both legs in white casts and in some type of contraption, lay her daughter. "I'll leave you two alone. Press the button if you need anything."

"Thank you." Sophia walked over and glanced at Katie. It was hard to be mad at her when she was in that condition. She was so thankful that her child was breathing, it was impossible to be mad at her. She leaned over and kissed her cheek. "Katie, it's Mom. Please wake up."

But there was no response. Katie slept as if she hadn't a care in the world.

Sophia sat by her daughter's bedside, holding her hand, wiping her forehead, and telling her stories. At night she slept on the small cot they had moved into the room. Several times Brad came, standing on the other side of the bed, staring at his daughter, but Sophia didn't speak to him. There was nothing to say. The doctors and nurses made their rounds, shaking their heads at her sleeping daughter. They still couldn't tell her why she wasn't waking up.

Sophia prayed, harder than she had ever prayed in her life, applying everything she had learned on the diva trail. She lit candles, chanted, and called upon the divas for help. But no one showed up to help her in her time of grief and despair.

She remembered Katie as a little girl, her first word, the thrill of watching her ride a two-wheel bicycle for the first time, and thought about their complex relationship. Katie had been a stubborn child, wanting to do everything her older brother did. Sophia recalled Katie's first birthday party, the many ballet recitals, and all the school functions she had gone to. Had she been a good enough mother? Had she loved her enough? Motherhood was demanding, constant, and required stamina. She sniffled as she remembered the miracle of birth and the boundless love and protectiveness she had felt for both of her babies.

Sophia thought about her own mother and realized that she had loved her in her own way. Now she understood how devastated her mother had been when her father had left her, and for the first time in her life realized that everything her mother had done was out of love. She just sucked at expressing it.

The days at the hospital passed slowly. Ben came home from school and spent time sitting with her by Katie's bedside. He found a job working construction. Sophia felt it was good for him. He was out in the fresh air all day and too tired at night to get into trouble.

One afternoon she fell asleep while reading to Katie. Brad gently shook her. "Let's get some coffee."

Sophia nodded, checked Katie, whose condition had not changed, and followed him downstairs. "Do you want something to eat?" She shook her head. She wasn't hungry; in fact, she hadn't really had a substantial meal in days. She could feel her pants slipping down her hips. What was the point of eating if her daughter died?

Brad led her over to a table in the corner. "What happens if she doesn't make it?" Sophia asked him.

"She will. The doctors know what they're doing." He apprised her. "You look amazing."

She laughed. "I guess that's what happens when you get rid of dead weight."

"I'm serious. What did you do to yourself?"

"I hiked, met some interesting women, and painted some pictures. I even sold one. And I wrote a book, too." She was tempted to tell him that she was involved with a younger man, but decided against it.

He raised his eyebrows. "Someone bought one of your pictures?"

"Yes. I'm quite talented, I'm told."

As she expected, Brad ignored her comment about her being told that she was talented. "I wanted to talk to you because I have a good offer on the house, and I think we should take it. These people are paying cash and want to close in two weeks. We both need to go forward."

The world tumbled down around her. She stared at her husband. Katie was lying upstairs in that bed and he wanted to sell the house now. "Can't it wait?"

He shook his head. "This is probably not the time to tell you, but Leslie and I are having a baby. We've already found a house we like, and she wants to get the baby's room ready."

Sophia studied him and wondered what she had ever seen in him? He was the most self-absorbed man on the planet. His daughter was lying upstairs, in serious condition, and he was worried about his new house. "I've heard the rumor." Sophia took a good sized gulp of her coffee then said, "Whatever."

"What does that mean?"

"It means—do what you want. You always have. I don't expect you to change now."

Brad, obviously uncomfortable with the way the conversation was heading, shifted around in his seat. "I don't mean to cause you any more pain, Sophia. I just have to think about Leslie and the baby."

"And what happens to Ben and Katie? Are they tossed aside because you have a new young wife and baby? How do you think they feel?"

He picked at his manicured cuticles. "Ben and Katie are fine with it. We've discussed it. I've agreed to your demands. The papers will be ready shortly. Selling the house will make the division of assets easier."

She felt a murderous rage as she stared at her *almost* ex-husband. She had to get away from him. "I don't think I want to finish this coffee or conversation with you. Sell the stupid house. Marry the child and have another one. I'll think of you when you're sitting out at the ball games and school functions in your sixties." She hurried away before she burst into tears.

* * *

Two weeks after, as Sophia sat by Katie's bedside, she heard a groan. "Katie, Katie. Are you there? It's Mom. Can you hear me?" Katie's eyelids fluttered as Sophia stroked her hand. "Katie, Katie."

Katie slowly opened her eyes. "Mommy," she whispered, then glanced around the room. "Where am I?"

Sophia hugged her gently, not wanting to hurt her bandaged ribs. "Everything's going to be okay, honey. You're fine. You're in the hospital. You were in an accident." She pressed the buzzer to summon the nurse.

Katie looked puzzled, then nodded. "I remember now. I was in Daddy's car …I'd been drinking, and … oh no, was anyone else hurt?"

"No honey, no one else was involved in the accident."

Tears made their way down the sides of Katie's cheeks. "Oh, Mom. I made a stupid mistake. I'm so sorry."

Sophia gently pushed hair away from Katie's cheek and rubbed her head gently. "We all make mistakes, sweetheart. It's going to be all right. *You're* going to be all right."

The nurse came into the room. "Well, young lady. You're back. Let me get the doctor. He's going to want to check you out."

"Is Daddy mad at me? Did I wreck his car?"

Sophia nodded. "The car is totaled, but that doesn't matter. We can discuss that later. The important thing is that you are okay."

"How long was I asleep?"

Sophia counted the days in her mind from that fateful phone call. "Fifteen days."

The nurse returned. "The doctor is on his way." She lifted Katie's arm and took her pulse. "You seem to be fine, young lady. You are one lucky girl."

Sophia's heels clicked on the floors as she walked around her former house, which felt unusually cold and sterile. Picking up several real estate calling cards, she wondered how many people had tromped through her home. *You're here to decide what you want*, she reminded herself as she walked through the rooms, making a list. *Hmm, the kids need their furniture. I've always liked the family room couch. I need my books and art supplies.*

She decided to take the kitchen table, but had no desire for the formal living room and dining room furniture. *Let*

Brad and Leslie have it. Taking a notepad from the kitchen counter, she labeled the items. As she was leaving, she heard a car drive up, and glanced out the window and saw Brad get out of a blue Taurus. She met him at the door.

"You were early," he said. "I thought you said five-fifteen."

She shrugged. "I needed to get a few things to take back to the motel room. I've labeled everything I want."

"You can stay here until the house closes. That would give you another week without paying rent."

She gave him a glaring look, straight into his eyes and said with strength and determination, "I don't want to be around this place. Besides, tomorrow I'm looking at a house to rent. I might be able to move in next week."

"I am sorry, Sophia. This whole thing just happened."

Even though she was trying as hard as she could, she had to bite her lip and pause a few moments before responding so she would not show the pain she felt. "Maybe our marriage was never meant to last a lifetime. We have two beautiful kids who both have problems at the moment. We need to act like their parents and guide them through this time. Katie is spoiled, Brad. We have to nip this before it gets any worse. Perhaps this was a wakeup call for all of us."

"I don't follow you."

"She could have been killed, Brad. She could have killed someone else. She's been indulged too much. Once she's recovered, she needs to get a job and earn her own spending money. She's wasted the semester, and I propose we don't send her back. She can go to the university here so we can keep an eye on her. And Ben, he's had some problems, too. He needs a father. You were never home for him."

"Let's not go there."

"I'm not trying to place blame. I just needed some help when they were growing up. I made some mistakes with the kids, but I'm not going to make any more. I will help Katie get back on her feet, but I expect some help from you."

"I will do my best."

Sophia smiled. "That's all I'm asking. She reached for her purse, staring at her *almost* former husband. He had put on weight since she had left, and the gray around his temples was more pronounced. He looked like he had aged ten years. "When's the baby due?"

"September twenty-second. They think it's twins."

She grinned wickedly. "Double the fun." She walked to the door. "I'll be in touch."

* * *

Through her contacts, Sophia was able to find a small cottage for rent. The owner, a professor of Archeology at the university, was taking a sabbatical and she was thrilled to rent her place to Sophia and her two grown children. She met the woman, Dr. Mary Harvey, at the cottage the following afternoon. "It's a pleasure meeting you," Dr. Harvey said. "I can't believe my good fortune. I've already interviewed several applicants and they're not what I'm looking for. I was about to leave the house vacant."

Sophia smiled warmly. She judged the woman to be in her early forties. She had brown hair tinged with gray that fell to her shoulders. "I will take wonderful care of your place, Dr. Harvey."

"Call me Mary, please. When someone calls me Dr. Harvey I always think they want me to look at their tonsils." She chuckled at her own remark a little before saying, "Let me show you around." Mary led Sophia around the bungalow. It had three bedrooms, two bathrooms, a large sunny living room, a kitchen, and a basement. "The house was built in 1943," Mary said as she led Sophia from room to room. "I've redone the house, but managed to keep its integrity." Mary ran her hand over the plaster walls. "The heat is oil, but you won't need to worry about that until fall," Mary added.

Sophia smiled as she stood in the entrance of the master bedroom. Sunshine spilled through the paned windows. There was an alcove where she could place her easel, and the view in the backyard was inspiring. "Who's the gardener?"

Mary blushed. "Me. I love gardening. It's my passion. But, I'm going to hire a service to keep it up while I'm gone."

Sophia studied the colorful flowerbeds, the carefully mowed lawn, and the large shade trees. "I'd be happy to take care of the yard. I always took care of ours. My son will mow the lawn and my daughter will enjoy sitting under the trees while she heals."

It was a beautiful day. The weather forecaster had predicted ninety degrees. Sophia lugged the last of the boxes into the cottage. She had managed to inter-mix the few things she had taken from her former life into Mary's decor. The taxi driver waited patiently at the curb with Mary's luggage already in the trunk.

"Oops, I forgot this," Mary said, holding up a folder as she walked toward Sophia. "It's my contacts in Greece. Sometimes I'm so absentminded." She stopped and held out her hand. "Thanks for showing up on my doorstep. I hope your children grow this summer. I never had children of my own, but I do work with college students and I know they can be difficult."

Sophia nodded in total agreement. Over the last few days she and Mary had become friends. "The universe works in mysterious ways," Sophia said. "I think we're going to love it here."

Mary got into the cab. "I'll be in touch. I'm due back in May." She motioned to cabdriver. "To the airport, please."

Sophia watched Mary drive away and thought about the recent good fortune that had befallen her. The house deal had closed; her bank account was thick. The divorce papers would be ready in a week. She giggled as she thought about Brad's new life. Leslie was extremely protective of him, not letting him visit the kids without her being there, too. *Does Leslie really think I want him back?*

Ben was working five days a week and staying out of trouble. Katie was out of the hospital and on the mend. Sophia had found a job at the art museum teaching painting to children, and now she had her new place. She heard the phone ring. Who would be calling her here? Only Brad and Cassandra had the number. She raced into the house. "Hello."

"Is this Sophia Roberts?" a woman's voice asked.

"Yes. What can I do for you?"

"This is Diane Hall from Mercy Hospital in Palm Springs. I've afraid I have some bad news. Your mother suffered a fatal heart attack early this morning."

"Fatal?"

"I'm sorry, Mrs. Roberts. There was nothing we could do for her."

Chapter 20

Ben couldn't get time off work and Katie wasn't fit to travel, so Sophia sent them to Brad's, packed a small bag, and boarded the plane. Cassandra was going to meet her in Palm Springs. Sophia took the early morning flight to Los Angeles, rented a small car and drove across the desert, following the directions Cassandra had given her. She arrived in the late afternoon, the sun shimmering on the asphalt. It was hot—damn hot, so she adjusted the air conditioning as high as it could go, the blast of cold air stinging.

She pulled up to her mother's home, turned off the car engine, and stared at the condo. *I should have been a better daughter. I should have visited more, and called her weekly.*

But they were two different people. Sophia glanced at her watch. Susan should be arriving shortly. It would be good to see her sister. It had been too long.

As she walked toward the front door, lugging her suitcase, a tanned wrinkled lady with white curls opened the door and waved. "You must be Sophia. I recognize you from a picture your mother has in her bedroom. I'm Gert, your mother's friend." She smiled softly. "Don't be sad, honey. Your mother went quickly. I only hope I'm that lucky. Your aunt called and said they're running late. You sister's plane was delayed because of weather. Why would anyone want to live in New Hampshire?"

"She likes it there because she's clear across the country," Sophia said as she followed Gert into the house, her heels clicking on the marbled floor. There were lush ferns gracing the front door and colorful artwork hung on the pale pink walls. She recognized her aunt's signature on several. Then she peered into the living room where she found brightly colored couches, white carpeting and walls filled with more artwork. *Good thing I never brought the children here*, she thought as she slipped off her shoes as not to dirty the pristine carpet. *Mother would have yelled at them not to dirty her clean floors.*

"I'll show you the bedrooms. Either you girls bunk together, or one of you sleeps in your mother's room. Your aunt's staying at a hotel because she thinks the two of you need to be alone and talk. She mentioned it's been awhile since you've seen each other."

"I'll take the guest room." *Susan could sleep with the ghost.* Sophia opened the door and threw her suitcase down on the queen-sized bed. The white shutters were partially opened, and she glimpsed at the golf course as she turned to the woman. "I'm going to take a nap. It's been a long day."

"Have a nice sleep."

"Hey, thanks for making me sleep in the old bat's room. Don't you remember how spooked I get?"

Sophia opened her eyes. Susan was standing next to the bed, her muscular arms on her hips, and a scowl on her face.

"It's great to see you." Sophia threw her arms around Susan, then pulled back and studied her. "It's been a while, Sis. You look great." Susan sat on the bed. There were faint lines around her lips and eyes, her hair still long and blond, but graying at the temples. She looked like she had gained weight. "Farm life must agree with you."

"It's the fresh air. You try getting up at five in the morning and milking those cows." Then Susan studied Sophia. "You look fabulous, Sophia. You've finally put on some weight." Her voice grew softer. "I'm sorry about your divorce."

Sophia laughed. "Did I tell you he's going to be a father again? Twins?"

Susan grinned. "Serves the asshole right. I never did like him. He was always a pompous prick." She scrunched her face. "Seriously, Sophia. Did you have a face lift or something? Botox? Because you look fantastic."

She smiled, wondering if she should tell Susan about the divas and Isis, but a voice whispered, *She's not ready. Give her time.* "It must be getting rid of Brad and all his stupid rules. Come on. Let's take a walk."

They strolled through the retirement community. Shadows crept along the mountains and the sounds of birds and insects filled the air. They caught up on their lives and when they had exhausted the subject, they made their way back to the condo. When the arrived, they found Cassandra sitting on the front step with a glass of wine in her hand. "I have something to show you girls. Come on inside."

They followed their aunt into the living room. Cassandra motioned for them to sit on the floral couch. She poured them wine and held up a thick packet. "This is your mother's last will and testament. I know what's in it because she called me once and told me. She wants you to sell the condo in Laguna and this one, split the proceeds, and divide her personal belongings between you two. She also has quite a bit of money in stocks. Even though your mother spent money like it was water, she was quite lucky in the stock market. I suggest you hang on to the stocks. Consider them your nest eggs for retirement." Cassandra placed the packet down on the glass table and picked up two pink sealed envelopes. "She left you these." Sophia took the sealed envelope her aunt had handed her, held it up to her nose and lingered a moment with the aroma of her mother's signature smell—Channel Number 5. "The viewing's tomorrow," Cassandra continued. "Your mother had the entire ordeal planned. Gert has given me the names of several real estate agents and I suggest you list the house before you return."

* * *

Sophia and Susan stood by the coffin, murmuring and accepting condolences from their mother's many friends. "I didn't know she had so many friends," Sophia whispered to her sister as she stared at her mother's body.

Susan burst into tears. "It doesn't even look like her. She would have never worn that color eye shadow. And her hair!"

Sophia hugged her sister. Glancing at her mother's body, she appeared to be sleeping, her over-processed hair teased and styled into a flip, eyes shadowed in light blue, and too much bright pink lipstick. Perhaps this was the standard look for dead matrons? Her mother wore an ivory linen suit. Several pieces of costume jewelry draped her thin neck and wrists. Sophia shuddered as she stared at the body. When she passed over, she planned to be cremated.

Finally, the last guests left and Sophia and Susan stood with Gert and Cassandra. "I never thought it would end," Sophia whispered to Gert. "Mother was certainly popular."

Gert smiled. "Yes she was. Funerals are social events here. People like attending because it reminds them that they are still alive. Your mother will be missed."

"Thanks for all your help, Gert," Cassandra said. "I'm going to take these girls home. They've had a long day. We'll see you tomorrow." Cassandra led them out to the car and whispered to Sophia, "There wasn't one woman in that group who had reclaimed her divine diva."

Sophia paused, remembering some of the conversations she had had with many of the women. "I guess you're right. I didn't think about it. They were more concerned about their social lives, housekeepers, and golf games."

"That's what happens to you if you don't take charge. That is why you wrote the book," Cassandra said.

"What book did you write? What's a divine diva? Is it some kind of new perfume?" Susan asked. "Is there something going on I need to know."

Sophia and Cassandra exchanged glances. "When it's your time, you will find out. I'll make sure of that," she told her sister.

"Whatever," Susan said. "I feel jet-lagged. Let's go back and get some sleep." They tumbled into Cassandra's car.

"I'll bring some coffee and rolls when I come to get you in the morning," Cassandra said. "The mortuary will have her at the gravesite. You girls held up well. I'm proud of you. I know how difficult this is."

* * *

The following morning Sophia stood between Cassandra and Susan at the gravesite, already the perspiration was trickling down her back. She struggled to listen as the minister described Mary's enthusiasm for life and the many friends she left behind. Sophia tried to concentrate, even chuckled at a few comments, remembering her mother's penchant for backyard parties, singing old show tunes at the top of her lungs, even though she couldn't carry a tune, those dry martinis she drank by the pitcher, bridge on lazy afternoons, and her trips to exotic places. Mary had always sent postcards describing the food and how overweight the people were. Sophia still didn't understand her mother's hang up. Weight had been the soapbox she stood on and preached about. But in a strange sort of way, she loved her. After all, she was her mother. Weren't you supposed to love your mother? But why had she been so difficult?

A familiar fragrance caught Sophia's nose. She sniffed. It was her mother's signature smell. She glanced around. There must be some other older woman wearing Channel Number 5. The smell grew stronger. She turned around and saw an apparition of her mother dressed in a hot pink suit, the same one she had worn when Susan graduated from college. Her white blond hair blew in the breeze. Her mother motioned for her to follow her over to a tree.

"I'm going to get some air," she whispered to Susan.

"You're white as a ghost. Are you okay?"

"I'll be right back." Sophia walked over to the tall tree and burst into tears. Her mother stood with her thin hands on her hips, her nails painted bright pink.

"Now why are you crying? Sophia? Stop it. I'm fine. And why am I wearing that god-awful suit? I bet Gert found it at the back of my closet. I should have donated it when I had the chance. I never did like it." She paused. "Well, it doesn't matter now. That's how all my friends will remember me." Her tone grew serious. "I want you to listen carefully because I don't have much time here. I'm sorry I screwed you and Susan up on that weight issue. I didn't want you both to be ridiculed because I was teased relentlessly by my father. He called me chubby in front of everyone. I did it for your own good. I didn't want you to ever be humiliated like I was. Now that I'm on the other side, I realize it probably wasn't as important as I thought it was, but I was human. What did you expect? Perfection? A saint?"

Sophia opened her mouth, but her mother shook her head, indicating that Sophia was not to speak. "I'm doing the talking now, and I want you to listen carefully. I apologize for not being the mother you wanted, but I tried my best. I really did. It's strange on the other side. Things are so much clearer. I see all my mistakes, and if I could do it over, I would, but they didn't give me that option. They only let me come back for a few blessed minutes to make my peace."

Sophia stared at her mother. Suddenly all the things she wanted to say about how she had ruined her life, the fact that she had been a poor grandmother didn't seem important. She was given a gift. A chance for closure. She remembered the lessons from the divas. "It's okay, Mom. Susan and I are going to be fine."

"I'm glad you're divorcing him. He is a jerk, and you deserve better. Thought he was better than all of us. He's not going to change, but you have. I see that. Susan needs your help. She's not as strong as you, and she's afraid to tell you she's having trouble with her marriage. Please watch over her." Her mother smiled. "My time is up. I have to go. Remember the good times. We had some."

She nodded, the tears stinging her eyes. "Yes we did, Mom."

"I do love you, Sophia. I am sorry for all the pain I caused." Sophia felt a breeze kiss her cheek, then the apparition vanished.

Sophia glanced around the cemetery. Her mother was gone. She gathered her composure, walked back to the crowd, and took her place next to Susan.

"Are you okay? You scared me. Do you want to sit down?" Susan asked.

Sophia blew her nose. "I'm fine. I just felt light-headed." She glanced over at Cassandra and winked, then focused on the minister's words.

"Whew, I'm glad that's over," Susan said as their mother's last friend left. The mourners had returned to the condo for finger foods and cocktails. Gert and several of her friends had organized the gathering.

Sophia's feet were killing her. She slid out of her high heels and flopped on the couch. "Now we have her things to go through, Susan. The real estate agent will be here at ten in the morning. That doesn't leave us much time."

Cassandra entered the room. "I have to leave now, girls. I have a large show next weekend, and I need to get ready." She kissed them. "I'll be in touch."

Susan hugged her aunt. "It was nice to see you, Cassandra. It's been too long. I'll try to get to Sedona for a visit." She turned to Sophia. "I'm going to change out of this dress. I'll be right back."

When Susan had left, Sophia turned to her aunt and threw her arms around her. "Thank you for everything you've done for me."

Cassandra smiled gently. "No—thank you. You've fulfilled your destiny. The lessons of the divas will soon be available for every woman."

"I haven't heard anything from the publisher Fran sent the book to. No one's going to want that story. I just threw it together."

"You underestimate yourself. Trust in the universe. You have been a marvelous student." Cassandra winked. "You will know what to do."

Gert poked her head into the room. "I'm leaving, ladies. It's been an emotional day for me. If you need something, my number is by the phone. There's a casserole one of your mother's bridge friends left on the counter, or you can go out." She smiled. "A night on the town might be just what you need. You know your mother would go out."

Sophia laughed. "Thanks, Gert. You've been a tremendous help."

Cassandra hugged Gert. "I'm on my way home, too. It was nice meeting you. I'm glad my sister had a friend like you."

"I'm going to miss Mary," Gert said. "Poker Tuesdays won't be the same without her."

Sophia changed out of her dress, then called home and checked on the kids. Leslie answered the phone. "Katie's sleeping and Ben's at work. Brad's not home yet. He's been putting in long hours at the office. The other night he didn't get home until eleven and I was stuck with your kids all night. I don't understand why he works so late. He has an assistant."

Sophia started to warn her about Brad's work habits, but held her tongue. "I'm sure it's just a big case. Tell the kids I called." She hung up.

"Hey, where are you?" Susan yelled. "You can't leave me with everything."

"Coming!"

They dragged the empty boxes into the living room. Sophia flipped on *West Side Story,* one of her mother's favorite musicals. "Do you want these?" she asked her sister as she held up several of their mother's antique teacups. Susan laughed. "We'll donate them."

When they finished, they pulled the boxes into their mother's bedroom and sorted through her extensive wardrobe. Sophia held up outfits for Susan's approval, but she shook her head. "I'm probably thirty pounds heavier than she was. Where would I wear them anyway? I live on a fucking farm."

"Are you okay?"

Susan burst into tears. "Bruce has someone else. I didn't want to tell you because you've been struggling with your own martial problems. He met her at a farm equipment show and they hit it off. She raises cattle in Wyoming and has been divorced for years. Bruce is selling the farm and has already filed for divorce. And all because of this woman and her cows!" She hiccupped. "I'm forty-five and I have nothing to show for myself. We never had kids. I let my career go to follow him to the wilds of New Hampshire and look where that got me!"

Sophia held her sister as she sobbed. "You're not a failure. This is Bruce's issue, not yours. I'll help you if you want, but first let's get out of here and get something to eat."

They decided on the Outback Steakhouse. "I'll have a martini," Susan told the hostess as she handed them the menus.

"I'd like a glass of chardonnay," Sophia said.

"I'll send your waitress right over," the young girl said as she lit their candle. "It won't be long."

They ordered, the drinks were served quickly, and they sipped as they discussed their upcoming divorces. "I guess we are like Mother after all," Susan commented. She downed her second martini. "I'll have another one," she said as she held her empty glass out to the waitress.

"I'll be right back. Are you ready to order?"

"After a few more drinks," Susan said as she leaned across the table. "So what do you think? Are we like her after all? God, the one thing I didn't want to be. My mother!"

"No, we're not," Sophia said. "Mother was negative and she attracted that energy. We're just going through a rough patch. You're welcome to come and live with me. I'd like the company."

Susan laughed. "No offense, Sis, but we haven't lived together since you left for college, and that was a long time ago. But I might come and visit for a few weeks. It's been years since I've been to the Sierras." She continued sipping her drink as she talked. "I'm thinking of going back to school. I want to pursue my doctorate. It's something I've always wanted to do, but Bruce didn't feel it was important. After we sell the farm and split the proceeds, I'll have quite a bit of money."

While sipping from her own glass of wine, Sophia studied her sister. Susan was Valedictorian of her high school class and graduated from UCLA with a perfect 4.0. She earned her masters degree in psychology the following year. "You were always good in school."

Susan twirled the liquid around in her glass. "School was easy for me because I knew that if I followed the syllabus and did the work I'd get the A." She shrugged. "I didn't always know what to expect at home. Mother was quite chaotic."

Sophia remembered her mother's erratic moods. "She could be a drama queen, that's for sure. Where do you want to go to graduate school?"

"I've already applied to several schools in the New York area. I want to live in the city again. I've had it with farm life and getting up before the sun does. I want lights and action."

Their dinners were served and Sophia dug in, amazed at how hungry she was. Conversation was light. They had said all they needed to say. When they finished and the plates were cleared, Sophia reached for the bill. Susan grabbed it first. "I have Bruce's card. He'll pay."

Sophia laughed. They were sisters after all.

A little after eleven that evening, Sophia said, "I'm taking a walk. I can't sleep.

Susan was sprawled on the couch watching a cable TV movie. "I don't think you have to worry about being attacked here in old folks central."

Sophia laughed. "I don't know. An old man might come after me with his cane."

The full moon cast its silvery light across the sidewalk. The desert air was cool and refreshing so Sophia took off across the golf course. Images of her mother flooded her mind: Mary laughing, drinking, waving her manicured hands around with gobs of flashy jewelry. She remembered going to war with her mother the year she turned thirteen. Her mother had started in on her that year about her weight, and every time she said one of her snide comments, it made Sophia eat all the more. She remembered pretending she was an orphan, walking behind her mother when they went out in public, and snickering unkind remarks. Each week she went to confession, plead guilty to her sins, then walked out of the confessional ready to commit them again. Looking back on her teenage years, she realized she probably needed help, but not the help that was offered to her in a confessional.

Sophia sat on a wooden bench and closed her eyes. She was so tired. Fingering the bracelet given by Ruby she still wore around her wrist, she closed her eyes and allowed the memories to dance across her mind. She felt a strong breeze and heard a humming sound and her name whispered. The sound of harps took her away from her thoughts and she opened her eyes to the apparition of a heavenly woman cloaked in the radiance of the sun. Sophia gasped—it was the same woman from the church in Sedona. The woman smiled benevolently, rays of pink and white shooting off in various directions. "I have a gift for you, Sophia. Please close your eyes."

Sophia shivered as she gazed into the woman's blue eyes. She nodded, closed her eyes, and witnessed her life. She saw her mother tending her as a baby, kissing her scraped knees when she had been a clumsy toddler, making her feel special when Susan arrived. She saw the three of them dancing around the living room to show tunes, the wacky birthday parties her mother had thrown for her. She saw her mother's attempts at consoling her after a bad date, a horrible perm, and the rejection from her first college choice. As the tears streamed down Sophia's cheeks, she realized that her mother had tried the best she could and that her issues of weight were due to her own fears. Her mother had always loved her. She opened her eyes and looked at the woman through her tears. The woman caressed her face. "Everything's going to be fine."

The woman floated up into the air, saying, "Do not grieve for your mother. She is with all the other mothers who have gone before her. Her work was done. She loved you the best way she knew how. You are still needed as a mother. Your children need your guidance, your sister needs your wisdom, and the world needs your vision. A diva shows compassion to those who ache. She helps others accept their loss. She gives back to others. Your children are grieving over the loss of your marriage and they need you." She winked. "Kurt can wait." The heavenly woman floated back down and kissed her tenderly on the cheek.

Sophia was up before Susan the next morning. She padded into the kitchen, made coffee, watered her mother's houseplants, and took the letter that her aunt had given her from her robe pocket. It was time to read it. Her fingers trembled as she opened the envelope and sat at the table.

Dear Sophia,
If you're reading this letter, then the eventual has occurred, and I am no longer of this earth. Already I miss the physical comforts. But I am not afraid. It is my turn. I have been on this planet for seventy-five years, and for the last five years, my health hasn't been good. Oh, I know what you're going to say. I should have quit smoking. I tried many times, but never stuck to it. It was one of the physical pleasures I enjoyed. I haven't told you and Susan about my health problems, because I didn't want to burden you. It's my heart. It's giving out. My arteries are clogged and one of the valves is shot. My lungs are going and my doctor tells me that it won't be long before I have to drag around one of those damn oxygen tanks. And that is something I never want to do! He warned me about my habits, and suggested surgery, but you know me. I love my cigarettes and martinis. I don't have time to lie around in bed.

I know about the journey. Cassandra tried many times to get me to take it, but I was too busy. It didn't fit in with my golf and bridge commitments. I regret it now. Oh, I know what you're thinking. I could have taken it at any time, but I didn't. You know me. That kind of stuff makes me feel uncomfortable.

I'm sorry if I disappointed you as your mother. I do love you. Take care of your sister and make sure she takes the journey so she doesn't end up like me. Tell your children I'm sorry I wasn't a better grandmother. It had nothing to do with them. It was me.

Love, Mom

Sophia burst into tears as Susan stumbled into the kitchen. "Coffee, great," she said as she poured a cup and sat across from her. "Why are you crying?"

She shoved the letter at her sister. Susan read it, her eyes darting across the page. "What's this journey?"

Smiling gently, Sophia said, "When you're fifty, I'll tell you all about it."

"Yikes—fifty. That's old." She covered her mouth, hoping to avoid a giggle slipping out. "Sorry, Sophia. That was mean."

Sophia reached for her sister's hand. "It's okay. I used to feel that way, but I've changed. I'm sorry I haven't been a better big sister. Let's put the past behind us and take an adventure this year. We'll work around your school schedule."

"Okay. I could do that." Her face grew serious. "What happens if I don't get accepted?"

"Of course you will. You were always the smart one."

"And you were the artistic one. Where shall we go?"

"Spain? Italy?"

Susan smiled. "I could handle that. Just the two of us?"

"Yep, I'll make sure Brad's available to keep an eye on Ben and Katie. Besides, he'll be around changing diapers anyway."

Sophia drove to the car-rental return, turned the car in, took the bus to the terminal, and stood in line in the maze for a security screening. She stripped off her belt, slid her shoes off, and when the buzzer beeped, she removed her watch and bracelet. She was pulled aside by a security person, the wand moving around her body, and finally was allowed to put her things back on. Glancing at her watch, she realized she was going to miss her flight, so she ran to the gate.

When she was finally on board, her seatback in its upright position, and her tray table latched, she closed her eyes and thought about her children. They were ready for her to come home. Katie complained that Leslie was moody. Ben said her cooking sucked and she was acting like a warden, and Brad seemed to want to talk to her. That was funny. They were due in the lawyer's office on Friday to sign the divorce papers. Perhaps a fifty-year-old woman looked better than a twenty-eight-year old woman carrying twins.

She remembered Cassandra's sage advice at the funeral: "A divine diva keeps her psyche uncluttered. She finds the space in her life for solitude and reflection. Life is short and she understands this. She honors the path of every person she encounters and allows him or her to explore life themselves without judgment. If you love yourself, then you will create abundance in your life. It is up to you—it is your life."

About The Author

Catherine MacDonald graduated from the University of the Pacific with a B.A. in English and a Minor in Communication Arts. She holds a Masters Degree in Education from the University of Nevada. Catherine is a former elementary school teacher in the Washoe County School District and taught a variety of English, Reading, and Literature classes at Truckee Meadows Community College. Catherine created the first novel writing course at the school and taught *The Artist Way* in Community Education. She was the Vice-President of the Romance Writers of Northern Nevada before it disbanded in 2002. Catherine is the author of *Reaching the Summit, The Jeweled Path, Road Queens,* and *Coming Home.*

After her youngest child left for college, Catherine resigned from Truckee Meadows Community College to go into business with her husband, Paul. Catherine and Paul own Sierra RV, a full-service dealership offering sales, service, parts, and rentals. Cathie began appearing on TV and radio with her dog Jack as *The RV Lady,* offering tips and information on the RV lifestyle. Catherine and Paul are the parents of two grown children. They reside in Reno, Nevada.

LaVergne, TN USA
07 July 2010
188675LV00001B/71/A